DATA VISUALIZATION
Using
POWER BI

AUTHORS

Mr. Chennaiah Kate, M.Tech(Ph.D)
Assistant Professor, Dept. Of CSE
St. Peter's Engineering College, Hyderabad

Mr. Siva Prasad V, M.Tech(Ph.D)
Assistant Professor, Dept. Of CSE
St. Peter's Engineering College, Hyderabad

Mr.Vijaya Raju Madri, M.Tech(Ph.D)
Assistant Professor, Dept. Of CSE
St. Peter's Engineering College, Hyderabad

ISBN: 979-83-3835-102-4

FIRST EDITION 2024

PREFACE

Welcome to "Data Visualization using Power BI"! In today's data-driven world, the ability to effectively visualize and interpret data is more crucial than ever. This book is designed to guide you through the essentials of Power BI, one of the most powerful tools available for data analysis and visualization.

What to Expect

In this book, we will explore the fundamentals of Power BI, ensuring that you develop a solid foundation in the principles of data visualization. We will start with the basics, covering the installation process for Power BI Desktop, and then progress to more advanced topics that will enable you to design compelling visuals.

Syllabus Overview

1. **Fundamentals of Power BI**:
   We will begin with an introduction to Power BI, exploring its key features and capabilities. You'll learn about its components, including Power BI Desktop, Power BI Service, and Power BI Mobile, as well as how these elements work together to create a seamless data analysis experience.

2. **Power BI Desktop Installation**:
   A step-by-step guide to installing Power BI Desktop will be provided, ensuring you have the necessary setup to begin your journey. This section will also cover system requirements and common troubleshooting tips to help you get started smoothly.

3. **Designing Visuals using Power BI Desktop**:
   The heart of this book lies in designing impactful visuals. You'll learn how to create a variety of visualizations, from simple bar charts to complex interactive dashboards. We'll discuss best practices for data representation, the importance of storytelling with data, and how to customize your visuals to enhance user engagement.

Who This Book is For

Whether you are a business analyst, data scientist, or a professional looking to enhance your data visualization skills, this book caters to all levels of expertise. No prior experience with Power BI is required, making it an excellent resource for beginners and a valuable refresher for more experienced users.

Why Power BI?

Power BI stands out for its user-friendly interface and powerful analytical capabilities, allowing users to transform raw data into insightful visualizations effortlessly. As organizations increasingly rely on data-driven decision-making, mastering Power BI will position you at the forefront of this trend.

Conclusion

As you embark on this journey through "Data Visualization using Power BI," I encourage you to engage with the material, practice the techniques presented, and explore the possibilities that data visualization offers. Together, we will unlock the potential of your data, transforming it into actionable insights that can drive meaningful change.

Let's get started on this exciting adventure of data visualization!

Mr. Chennaiah Kate

ACKNOWLEDGMENT

Writing "Data Visualization using Power BI" has been an incredible journey, and I am deeply grateful to all those who contributed to its completion.

First and foremost, I would like to extend my heartfelt thanks to my family for their unwavering support and encouragement. Your belief in me has been a constant source of motivation.

I am also grateful to my colleagues and friends who shared their insights and feedback throughout the writing process. Your expertise and perspectives have enriched this book and helped refine my ideas.

A special thank you goes to the Power BI community for their vibrant discussions and shared knowledge. Your passion for data visualization inspired me and provided countless resources that informed the content of this book.

I would also like to acknowledge the teams at Microsoft for developing such a powerful tool in Power BI. Your dedication to improving data accessibility has made it easier for users around the world to harness the power of their data.

Finally, to the readers: thank you for your interest in this book. I hope it serves as a valuable resource on your journey to mastering data visualization. Your desire to learn and grow in this field motivates me to continue sharing knowledge and insights.

Thank you all for being a part of this endeavor!

Mr. Chennaiah Kate

Table of Contents

Chapter 1: Fundamentals of Data Visualization 1

    1.1 Data Visualization 1

    1.2 Characteristics of Effective Data Visualization 1

    1.3 Why need Data Visualization 2

    1.4 Importance of Data Visualization 2

    1.5 Benefits of Data Visualization 3

    1.6 Techniques for Effective Data Visualization 4

    1.7 Future Trends in Data Visualization 4

    1.8 Where Data Visualization Use 5

    1.9 Types of Data for Visualization 5

    1.10 Stages of Decision-making Using Data Visualization 6

Chapter 2: Introduction of Power BI 7

    2.1 What is a Power BI 7

    2.2 Importance of Data Visualization 8

    2.3 What is Power BI used for? 8

    2.4 Who uses Power BI? 9

    2.5 Why Power BI? 10

    2.6 Power BI Products 12

    2.7 Power BI Desktop 15

    2.8 Power BI Visual Elements 23

    2.9 Power BI Architecture 41

    2.10 What is a Power BI Service? 44

    2.11 Power BI Service Architecture 45

    2.12 Power BI Dashboard 47

Chapter 2: Installation of Power BI Desktop 50

    2.1 Downloading Power BI Desktop 50

    3.2 Power BI Desktop Installation 52

    3.3 Launch Power BI Desktop 57

    3.4 Power BI Desktop Window Icons and Buttons 60

Chapter 4: Creating Visuals With Power BI 67

Chapter 1: Fundamentals of Data Visualization

Human minds are more adaptive to visual representations of data than textual data. We can easily understand things when they are visualized. It is better to represent the data through a graph, where we can analyze the data more efficiently and make specific decisions according to data analysis.

1.1 Data Visualization

Data visualization is the graphical representation of information and data. It involves the use of visual elements like charts, graphs, maps, and dashboards to help people understand complex data sets quickly and easily. By presenting data visually, it highlights trends, patterns, and outliers, making it easier for viewers to grasp insights and make informed decisions. Effective data visualization transforms raw data into an accessible and engaging format, facilitating communication and understanding across various audiences.

Graphics provides an excellent approach for exploring the data, which is essential for presenting results. Data visualization is a new term. It expresses the idea that involves more than just representing data in the graphical form (instead of using textual form). This can be very helpful when discovering and getting to know a dataset and help classify patterns, corrupt data, outliers, and much more. With a little domain knowledge, data visualizations can be used to express and demonstrate key relationships in plots and charts. The static does indeed focus on quantitative description and estimations of data. It provides an important set of tools for gaining a qualitative understanding.

What is Data visualization – It is an activity that involves collecting unstructured data from various sources, modeling it, and displaying it in an organized and readable manner thus aiding better decision-making. It presents the data using visuals like interactive graphs and charts, making information more compelling and easier to interpret for all types of users.

The primary goal of data visualization is to make data more accessible and easier to interpret, allowing users to identify patterns, trends, and outliers quickly. This is particularly important in the context of big data, where the sheer volume of information can be overwhelming without effective visualization techniques.

1.2 Characteristics of Effective Data Visualization

1. **Clarity:** Visualizations should present data clearly, allowing viewers to quickly understand the main insights without confusion.
2. **Relevance**: The data displayed should be pertinent to the audience's needs and context, focusing on what matters most.
3. **Simplicity**: Strive for a straightforward design that avoids unnecessary complexity, making the information easy to digest.
4. **Accuracy**: Represent the data truthfully, ensuring that visuals do not distort or mislead viewers.
5. **Interactivity**: Incorporating interactive elements allows users to explore the data, enhancing engagement and facilitating deeper insights.
6. **Aesthetics**: A visually appealing design can attract attention and maintain interest, but it should not sacrifice clarity.
7. **Scalability**: Effective visualizations should work well with different data sizes and types, remaining clear and informative.

8. **Consistency**: Use consistent colors, fonts, and styles throughout the visualization to create a cohesive understanding.
9. **Insightful**: Beyond just showing data, effective visualizations should help users draw conclusions and make informed decisions.
10. **Context**: Providing context or annotations can help viewers understand the significance of the data and its implications.

These characteristics work together to ensure that data visualizations are not only informative but also engaging and useful for the audience.

1.3 Why need Data Visualization

Data visualization helps to tell stories by curating data into a form easier to understand, highlighting the trends and outliers. A good visualization tells a story, removing the noise from data and highlighting useful information. Data visualization is essential for several reasons:

1. *Simplifies Complex Data*: Raw data can be overwhelming and difficult to interpret. Visualization breaks it down into a more understandable format, making it easier to grasp trends and patterns.
2. *Enhances Understanding*: Visual representations—like charts, graphs, and maps—allow people to quickly comprehend relationships within the data, making insights more accessible.
3. *Identifies Trends and Patterns:* By visualizing data, you can easily spot trends, correlations, and anomalies that might be missed in raw data. This helps in making data-driven decisions.
4. *Facilitates Communication*: Data visualization is an effective way to convey information to others, whether in reports, presentations, or dashboards. Visuals can bridge gaps in understanding among different audiences.
5. *Encourages Exploration*: Interactive visualizations allow users to dive deeper into the data, exploring different dimensions and uncovering insights on their own.
6. *Supports Decision-Making*: Visualizations provide clear evidence and insights, aiding stakeholders in making informed decisions based on the data.
7. *Improves Retention*: People tend to remember visual information better than text-based data. Effective visualizations can enhance recall and understanding over time.
8. *Engagement*: Well-designed visuals can capture attention and engage viewers, making data more interesting and relevant.

Data visualization transforms complex data into clear, actionable insights, making it a crucial tool in fields ranging from business and science to education and journalism.

1.4 Importance of Data Visualization

8 Big reasons why data visualization is important for any business
1. Determining performance over a period
2. Understanding customer sentiment
3. Ease of data analysis
4. Seamless data presentation
5. Interpreting correlations in relationships
6. Analyzing risk
7. Identifying patterns
8. Analyzing and predicting trends

- *Understanding Complex Data*

To begin with, in an era of big data, understanding complex datasets is a monumental task. In order to make the Data more comprehensible and useful, Data visualization simplifies it by converting intricate data into visual representations that are easy to interpret and comprehend. It allows us to identify patterns, trends, outliers, and relationships that might be hidden in raw data and not easily visible otherwise.

- ***Improved Decision-Making***

It is unequivocally clear that informed decisions are always based on solid data and visually comprehensible data is always easy to digest and interpret. By presenting data visually, decision-makers can quickly grasp the key points and make more accurate, more informed, and timely decisions. This is true for almost every sector of life, however especially important in business, healthcare, and government sectors.

- ***Effective Communication of Insights***

To its credit, Data visualization is a powerful storytelling tool that helps in conveying insights and trends to both technical and non-technical audiences. These insights can then be effortlessly and conveniently made into more useful information. By creating engaging visuals, you can ensure that your message is not only comprehensible with ease but also is understood and remembered more valuably.

- ***Identifying Patterns and Trends***

Patterns and trends are of monumental importance in any business and are often elusive in raw data. But when the patterns and trends are represented in a visually appealing way, they are enormously valuable because visualization makes it easier to spot them, helping businesses and researchers uncover valuable insights and make data-driven predictions. It goes without saying that provided with the in-vogue patterns and trends, businesses can capitalize on what is needed and more important.

1.5 Benefits of Data Visualization

Data visualization offers a multitude of highly valuable benefits. Amongst many, some of the most availing benefits are discussed below:

- ***Enhanced Comprehension***

It is a known fact that visual representations are processed faster by the human brain than raw data. This leads to better comprehension and retention of information, making it an invaluable tool for educators, analysts, and decision-makers.

- ***Increased Engagement***

Comparatively, visuals are more engaging and memorable than lengthy reports or spreadsheets for they captivate the audience and make the information more relatable and accessible. Thus, visual data has the potential to attract more engagement.

- ***Data-Driven Storytelling***

Data visualization has the potential to weave narratives around data. Consequently, this not only simplifies complex information but also engages the audience, making it easier to convey a compelling and engaging story.

- ***Improved Data-Driven Strategies***

It is beyond contention that data-driven strategies are essential for businesses today like never before because effective data visualization enables organizations to identify growth opportunities, optimize operations, and adapt to changing market conditions.

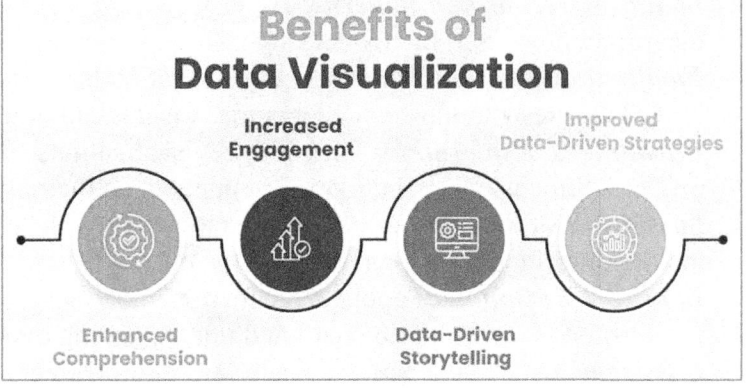

1.6 Techniques for Effective Data Visualization

Having gotten a good grasp of the importance and benefits of data visualization, now it is time to explore some of the effective data visualization techniques for a better outcome. To this end, creating impactful data visualizations involves careful planning and execution. Here are some key techniques that are to be considered in this regard:

- *Choosing the Right Visualization Type*

Choose the most fitting visualization style. Primarily, the choice of visualization type depends on the data and the message you want to convey. There are various forms of it including bar charts, line graphs, pie charts, heat maps, and more. Always go with the one that best suits your data and perfectly aligns with your goals.

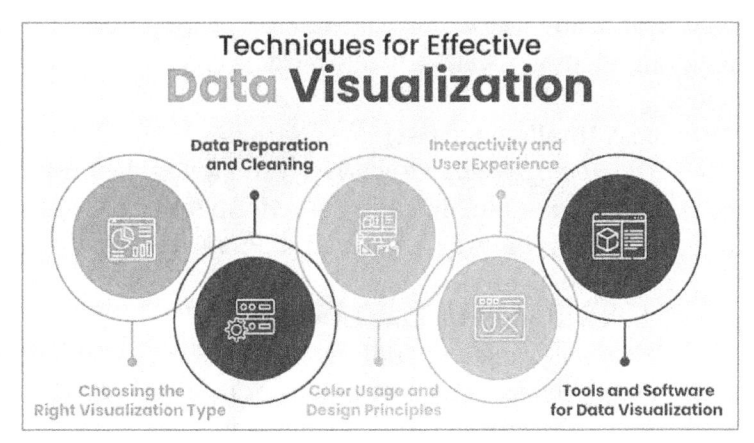

- *Data Preparation and Cleaning*

The quality of data is not to be compromised at any cost. So, ensure your data is accurate and relevant. For robust and high-quality data, cleaning and preprocessing are often required to remove outliers and inconsistencies. To this end, just remember that an elaborate pre-thought is much more availing than days of labor afterward.

- *Color Usage and Design Principles*

From a design and aesthetics perspective, effective use of color and design principles can make or break a visualization. Therefore, it is advisable to choose colors that convey the intended message and ensure the design is easy to comprehend, user-friendly, and aesthetically pleasing.

- *Interactivity and User Experience*

Interactive visualizations come with the luxury of allowing users to explore data on their terms which fosters increased user experience. It is, therefore, highly recommended to consider adding filters, zoom options, and tooltips for a richer user experience.

- *Tools and Software for Data Visualization*

There are numerous tools and software available to create data visualizations and it is important to choose the best one. Amongst scores of them, some popular options include Tableau, Power BI, Python libraries like Matplotlib and Seaborn, and web-based tools like D3.js.

1.7 Future Trends in Data Visualization

The field of data visualization is constantly evolving, and it is likely to undergo a tremendous transformation in the times to come. Here are some future trends to watch out:

- *Artificial Intelligence and Automation*

AI will play a significant role in automating the creation of data visualizations by providing real-time and more profound insights into various trends and patterns.

- *VR and AR Data Visualization*

Virtual Reality (VR) and Augmented Reality (AR), the quintessential game changers, will open up new dimensions in data visualization, offering immersive and interactive experiences.

- *Accessibility and Inclusivity*

Ensuring that data visualizations are accessible to all, including people with disabilities, will become a growing priority and gradual reality.

1.8 Where Data Visualization Use
Data visualization is widely used across various fields to make data more accessible and understandable by converting complex data sets into visual representations. Some common areas where data visualization is used include:

1. Business Intelligence (BI)
- *Dashboards and Reports*: Visualizing key performance indicators (KPIs), sales trends, financial summaries, etc., in an intuitive format like charts, graphs, and heatmaps for decision-making.
- *Market Analysis*: Understanding customer behavior, market segmentation, and competitive landscape using visual tools.

2. Data Science and Machine Learning
- *Exploratory Data Analysis (EDA)*: Understanding data distribution, relationships, and patterns through plots such as scatter plots, histograms, box plots, and correlation matrices.
- *Model Interpretability*: Visualizing model predictions, feature importance, and errors to improve model performance and interpretability.

3. Healthcare
- *Patient Data*: Visualizing patient history, vital signs, and treatment outcomes for better diagnosis and treatment planning.
- *Epidemiology*: Tracking the spread of diseases through maps and trend lines, especially useful during pandemic monitoring.

4. Finance
- *Stock Market Trends*: Plotting stock prices, volatility, and technical indicators to inform trading strategies.
- *Risk Management*: Visualizing potential risk factors, portfolio performance, and predictive models in financial planning.

5. Government and Policy
- *Public Data Visualization*: Making census data, public expenditures, or election results understandable to the public through visual reports and maps.
- *Policy Impact*: Visualizing the effects of public policies on the economy, health, or the environment.

6. Education
- *Student Performance*: Visualizing grades, attendance, and progress to identify trends in student learning.
- *Learning Analytics*: In educational software, data visualization is used to understand learning behaviors and engagement.

7. Marketing and Sales
- *Customer Segmentation*: Visualizing demographic data to tailor marketing campaigns.
- *Sales Performance*: Understanding sales pipelines, revenue trends, and conversion rates using charts and dashboards.

8. Geospatial Analysis
- *Maps and Spatial Data*: Visualizing geographic data, for example in logistics, city planning, or tracking environmental changes.

9. Social Media and Web Analytics
- *User Behavior*: Visualizing website or app traffic, engagement metrics, and user demographics.
- *Social Networks*: Displaying relationships and interactions within a network using graph visualization techniques.

Data visualization helps in identifying trends, uncovering insights, and making data-driven decisions efficiently across all these domains.

1.9 Types of Data for Visualization
Performing accurate visualization of data is very critical to market research where both numerical and categorical data can be visualized, which helps increase the impact of insights and also helps in reducing the risk of analysis paralysis. So, data visualization is categorized into the following categories:

- Numerical Data
- Categorical Data

Let's understand the visualization of data via a diagram with its all categories.

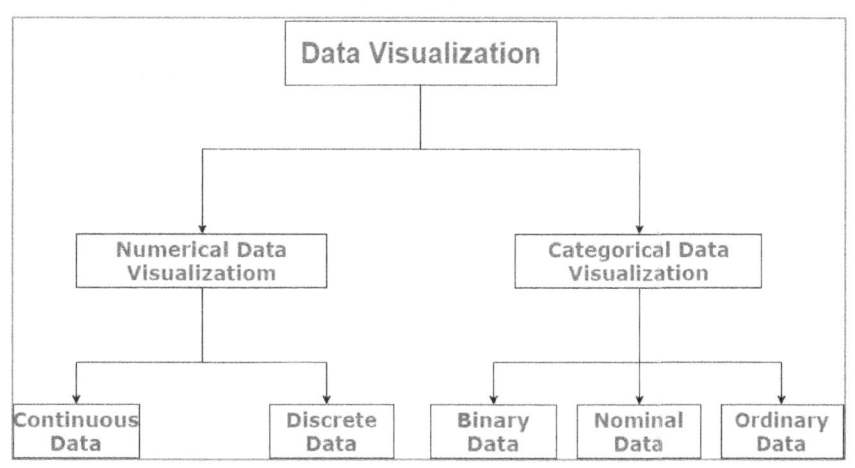

1. **Numerical Data :**
   Numerical data is also known as Quantitative data. Numerical data is any data where data generally represents an amount such as height, weight, age of a person, etc. Numerical data visualization is easiest way to visualize data. It is generally used to help others to digest large data sets and raw numbers in a way that makes it easier to interpret into action. Numerical data is categorized into two categories:
   - *Continuous Data* –It can be narrowed or categorized (For example, Height measurements).
   - *Discrete Data* –This type of data is not "continuous" (for example: Number of cars or children a household has).

   The type of visualization techniques that are used to represent numerical data visualization is Charts and Numerical Values. Examples are Pie Charts, Bar Charts, Averages, Scorecards, etc.

2. **Categorical Data**
   Categorical data is also known as Qualitative data. Categorical data is any data where data generally represents groups. It simply consists of categorical variables that are used to represent characteristics such as a person's ranking, a person's gender, etc. Categorical data visualization is all about depicting key themes, establishing connections, and lending context. Categorical data is classified into three categories :
   - *Binary Data* –In this, classification is based on positioning (Example: Agrees or Disagrees).
   - *Nominal Data* –In this, classification is based on attributes (Example: Male or Female).
   - *Ordinal Data* –In this, classification is based on ordering of information (Example: Timeline or processes).

1.10 Stages of Decision-making Using Data Visualization

There are four phases which are essential to decide for the organization:

- *Visualize:* We analyze the raw data, which means it makes complex data more accessible, understandable, and more usable. Tabular data representation is used where the user will look up a specific measurement, while the chart of several types is used to show patterns or relationships in the data for one or more variables.
- *Analysis:* Data analysis is defined as cleaning, inspecting, transforming, and modeling data to derive useful information. Whenever we make

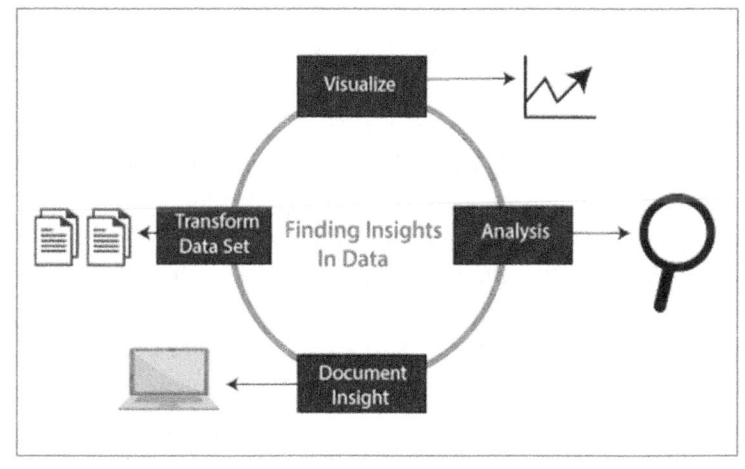

a decision for the business or in daily life, is by past experience. What will happen to choose a particular decision, it is nothing but analyzing our past. That may be affected in the future, so the proper analysis is necessary for better decisions for any business or organization.
- ***Document Insight:*** Document insight is the process where the useful data or information is organized in the document in the standard format.
- ***Transform Data Set:*** Standard data is used to make the decision more effectively.

Chapter 2: Introduction of Power BI

2.1 What is a Power BI

The full form of Power BI is *Power Business Intelligence.* Microsoft Power BI is an interactive data visualization software product developed by Microsoft with a primary focus on business intelligence. It is part of the Microsoft Power Platform. Power BI a set of software tools and connectors that help you transform data from multiple sources into actionable insights. Power BI is a collection of software services, apps, and connectors that work together to turn your unrelated sources of data into coherent, visually immersive, and interactive insights. Your data might be an Excel spreadsheet, or a collection of cloud-based and on-premises hybrid data warehouses. Power BI lets you easily connect to your data sources, visualize and discover what's important, and share that with anyone or everyone you want.

Power BI tools enable businesses to integrate data from various sources, create visualizations, and identify trends and patterns. Custom visuals, simple data access, and cloud services are all provided by Power BI to enable businesses to obtain insightful information.

Power BI helps businesses use data to make better decisions:
- *What it is*

Power BI is a collection of software, apps, and connectors that help users turn data from different sources into visual insights.
- *How it works*

Power BI connects to a variety of data sources, including Excel sheets, databases, and cloud-based apps. Users can then aggregate, analyze, visualize, and share the data.
- *Who uses it*

Power BI is designed for non-technical business users. It has an intuitive user interface and integrates with other Microsoft products.
- *How to use it*

Power BI can be downloaded for Windows 10 or 11, or used as a mobile app for Windows, Android, and Apple iOS. There's also a version called Power BI Report Server for companies that want to keep their data and reports on-premises.
- *How it's used*

Businesses can use Power BI to improve their decision-making processes. For example, a financial institution might use Power BI to connect all its data sources so that business users and IT staff can develop reports

According to DOMO, over 2.5 quintillion bytes of data are generated every single day, and 90% of the data in this world has been created in the last two years. It is a tough task to manage this huge amount of data and make sense of all of it.So, the majority of organizations are using Business Intelligence Visualization tools to derive value from data. Among these, *Power BI is one of the best visualization tools* to handle the data in distinct patterns and make observations. Data proliferation can be managed as part of the data science process, which includes data visualization. Using different **Power BI visuals or chart types** in *2023*, you can manage a vast amount of data quickly and effectively.

2.2 Importance of Data Visualization

We are inherently in the visual world where pictures or images speak more than words. So it is easy to visualize a large amount of data using graphs and charts than depending on reports or spreadsheets.

Data visualization is a quick and easy way to convey concepts to the end-users, and you can do experiments with different scenarios by making slight changes. It can also:
- Clarifies which element influences customer behavior.
- Identifies the area to which you need to pay attention.
- Guides you to understand which product should be placed in which location.
- Predicts the sales volume.

The better you visualize your points, the better you can leverage the information to the end-users.

You might have confusion regarding selecting the correct data visualization for the data sets you have. The right data visualization helps you to boost the impact of your data. Business Intelligence platforms like Power BI help in dealing with the different visualizations of data sets in a secure manner.

2.3 What is Power BI used for?

Whether you're a data pro or are just entering the business world, Power BI is designed to empower you with data-driven insights. You can use Power BI in a variety of ways, across industries and teams and functions within an organization. Let's explore some common uses for the platform include:

Data visualization and reporting
- Create reports and dashboards that present data sets in multiple ways using visuals.
- Turn data into a wide range of different visuals, including pie charts, decomposition trees, gauge charts, KPIs, combo charts, bar and column charts, and ribbon charts—among many other options.
- **Example**: A marketing team uses Power BI to create interactive dashboards that visualize campaign performance metrics. They can track metrics like click-through rates, conversion rates, and customer demographics, allowing them to quickly see which campaigns are effective.
- **Example**: A finance department generates monthly financial reports in Power BI. They compile data from various sources, such as sales and expenses, and present it in clear charts and graphs, making it easy for stakeholders to understand the company's financial health.

Data integration

- Connect various data sources, such as Excel sheets, onsite data warehouses, and cloud-based data storage, and then transform them into business insights.
- Integrate Power BI with a website.

Business intelligence
- Track key performance indicators (KPIs) and metrics in real time.
- Use built-in AI and machine learning to make business predictions based on historical data.
- **Example**: An IT team integrates data from multiple systems (like ERP, CRM, and Excel) into Power BI to create a unified view of the business. This consolidated data helps in identifying trends and making informed decisions
- **Example**: A retail manager utilizes Power BI to monitor store performance in real-time. The dashboard displays sales figures, inventory levels, and customer feedback, helping the manager make timely decisions about staffing and stock replenishment.

Collaboration and sharing
- Provide company-wide access to data, data visualization tools, and insights to create a data-driven work culture.
- Collaborate on workspaces and shared datasets.
- **Example**: A project team shares Power BI reports with stakeholders via the Power BI service, allowing everyone to access real-time data and insights. This enhances collaboration and ensures everyone is on the same page regarding project progress.

Financial analysis
- Create financial statements and balance sheets.
- Analyze sales performance and profit.
- **Example**: A healthcare provider uses Power BI to analyze patient data and predict admission rates based on historical trends, helping them allocate resources more efficiently.

Marketing and sales
- Integrate Power BI with a CRM system to analyze customer data and use insights to improve customer experience.
- Analyze market trends and consumer behavior to discover opportunities.
- **Example**: A product manager analyzes historical sales data using Power BI to identify seasonal trends. By visualizing this data, they can better forecast demand and adjust inventory and marketing strategies accordingly

2.4 Who uses Power BI?

Power BI users aren't limited to data professionals, such as data scientists or data engineers, and can include a wide range of different business users. In fact, the platform is intentionally designed so that non-technical users can easily create reports, manipulate data, and perform in-depth data analysis operations.

Nonetheless, some of the most common analyst positions that use the platform on a daily basis include the following:
- Business analysts
- Business intelligence analysts
- Supply chain analysts
- Data analyst

Power BI is utilized by various roles and industries for data visualization and analysis. Here are some specific examples:

1. **Business Analysts**:
   - **Example**: A retail company's business analyst uses Power BI to create dashboards that track sales performance across different regions, helping to identify trends and make informed decisions on inventory.
2. **Data Scientists**:

- **Example**: A data scientist at a tech firm employs Power BI to visualize complex datasets and present findings on user engagement, allowing the team to refine their product features based on user behavior.
3. **Executives and Managers**:
    - **Example**: A CEO of a manufacturing company uses Power BI to review an executive dashboard displaying key performance indicators (KPIs) such as production efficiency and revenue growth, facilitating strategic planning.
4. **IT Professionals**:
    - **Example**: An IT manager integrates various data sources into Power BI to monitor system performance and downtime, enabling quick responses to technical issues.
5. **Finance Teams**:
    - **Example**: A finance analyst uses Power BI to visualize monthly expenditure and revenue data, generating reports that help the finance team identify areas for cost reduction.
6. **Sales and Marketing Teams**:
    - **Example**: A marketing manager leverages Power BI to analyze campaign performance metrics, visualizing customer engagement data to optimize future marketing strategies.
7. **Healthcare Professionals**:
    - **Example**: A healthcare administrator uses Power BI to track patient outcomes and operational metrics, visualizing data to enhance service delivery and resource allocation.
8. **Education Administrators**:
    - **Example**: A university's registrar analyzes student enrollment and performance data with Power BI, using visualizations to identify trends and inform academic planning.

2.5 Why Power BI?

Reasons why Power BI is so popular and needed in the BI domain

1. Access to Volumes of Data from Multiple Sources

Power BI can access vast volumes of data from multiple sources. It allows you to view, analyze, and visualize vast quantities of data that cannot be opened in Excel. Some of the important data sources available for Power BI are Excel, CSV, XML, JSON, pdf, etc. Power BI uses powerful compression algorithms to import and cache the data within the .PBIX file.

2. Interactive UI/UX Features

Power BI makes things visually appealing. It has an easy drag and drops functionality, with features that allow you to copy all formatting across similar visualizations.

3. Exceptional Excel Integration

Power BI helps to gather, analyze, publish, and share Excel business data. Anyone familiar with Office 365 can easily connect Excel queries, data models, and reports to Power BI Dashboards.

4. Accelerate Big Data Preparation with Azure

Using Power BI with Azure allows you to analyze and share massive volumes of data. An azure data lake can reduce the time it takes to get insights and increase collaboration between business analysts, data engineers, and data scientists.

5. Turn Insights into Action

Power BI allows you to gain insights from data and turn those insights into actions to make data-driven business decisions.

6. Real-time Stream Analytics

Power BI will enable you to perform real-time stream analytics. It helps you fetch data from multiple sensors and social media sources to get access to real-time analytics, so you are always ready to make business decisions. Now, in this what is Power BI article, you will learn about the architecture of Power BI.

Features Of Power BI

In this section, we are going to look at the features that individuals and organizations can get when they decide to use Power BI.

1. Easy to set up: With Microsoft Power BI, you can get started in seconds. Signing up for the online service is FREE and you can take advantage of the simple, out of the box dashboards for common services like Salesforce, Google Analytics and Dynamics to start getting insights from your data in no time. You don't need to fill in
your credit card details as the only requirement for this service is a work or school email address.

2. Access your data wherever it is: With Power BI, it doesn't matter where your data is stored. Whether the data is stored in Excel spreadsheets, available online or resident in an on-premise database management system, you can still get a holistic view of the key metrics for your business from all the different sources.

3. Real Time reports: Microsoft Power BI offers interactive dashboards that display the changes to your data as they occur in real time. This means that you can notice trends, solve problems and seize opportunities as they occur. There are no more unnecessary delays with Power BI.

4. Ask questions and get answers: This is by far, one of my favorite features of Power BI. You can ask questions based on the data in your report and Power BI will provide you with the answers. It works similarly to a Google search. When you begin typing your questions, Power BI will give you suggestions on all possible questions that are similar to the one you are typing and that can be answered with the information contained in your report. Imagine asking a question like "What was last year's profit by product?" and getting the correct information provided to you visually. Power BI supports asking questions in a natural language, which in my opinion, is an awesome feature. Please note that at the time of writing this book, the only supported language for asking questions in Power BI is English.

5. Get everyone on the same page: Power BI provides organizations with a single view of the truth. This means that all stakeholders will have the current status of the business at every point in time. Power BI Groups allow you to collaborate with the key stakeholders of your business in order to make quick and confident decisions.

6. Make data-driven decisions from anywhere: Power BI gives you the ability to stay on top of your data, wherever you are. With touch-enabled native apps for Windows, iOS and Android, you can access all your data wherever you go. Gone are the days when business decisions were made only in the office. Welcome to the Power BI age.

7. Curated content just for your organization: With Power BI, you can create and publish content packs to your team or your entire organization. The content packs can include dashboards, reports
and datasets that provide every user with a personalized view of the business metrics that matter most to them.

8. Integrate your application or service with Power BI: Organizations can use the open, standards-based REST API to integrate their applications or services with Power BI, thus leveraging its rich and interactive reporting capabilities. This integration helps you deliver your solutions faster while focusing on your core values.

9. Share insights on your website or blog: With 'Power BI publish to web', organizations can create stunning visualizations and embed them on their websites within minutes. If your organization intends to share information like its annual reports in a visually engaging way on its website, from where your customers, partners, and shareholders can access it, using Power BI is a great way to achieve that.

Advantages Of Power BI

1. *User-friendly interface:* Power BI has an intuitive interface allowing users to visualize and analyze data easily.
2. *Data integration:* Power BI allows users to easily integrate data from various sources, including Excel, SQL Server, and cloud-based sources like Azure and Salesforce.
3. *Customizable dashboards:* Users can create customized dashboards and reports to display data in a way that is meaningful to them.
4. *Real-time data:* Power BI supports real-time data processing, which means users can view up-to-date data in their dashboards and reports.
5. *Collaboration:* Power BI allows users to share their dashboards and reports with others, making collaborating on data analysis projects easy.

Disadvantages Of Power BI
1. *Limited data processing capabilities*: Power BI is not designed for heavy-duty data processing and may struggle with large datasets or complex queries.
2. *Limited customization options:* While Power BI offers a range of customization options, users may find that they are limited in their ability to create truly unique visualizations and reports.
3. *Cost:* Power BI is not a free tool, and users may need to pay for additional features or storage space.

2.6 Power BI Products
Power BI products are also called as Power BI components or parts. Power BI consists of several products and services designed to help organizations analyze and visualize data effectively. These are designed to let you create, share, and consume business insights in the way that serves you and your role most effectively.

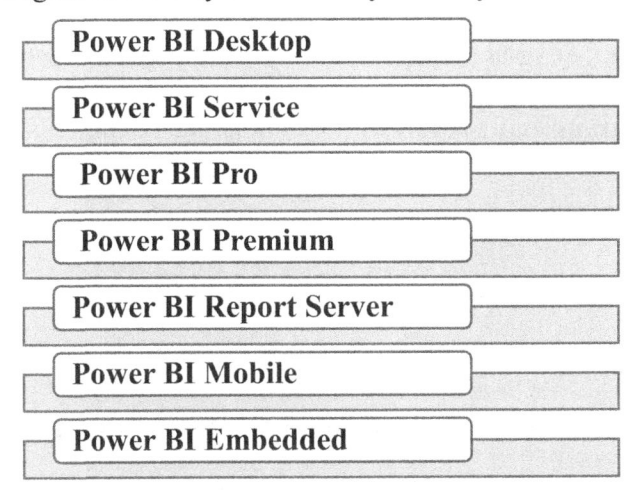

- Power BI Desktop
- Power BI Service
- Power BI Pro
- Power BI Premium
- Power BI Report Server
- Power BI Mobile
- Power BI Embedded

1. **Power BI Desktop**

A Windows desktop application called *Power BI Desktop*.
- **Overview**: A desktop application primarily used for creating reports and data visualizations.
- **Features**:
    - **Data Modeling**: Users can connect to multiple data sources, transform data, and create relationships between different datasets.
    - **Report Creation**: Drag-and-drop interface for building interactive reports with various visualizations like charts, graphs, and maps.
    - **Data Transformation**: Built-in tools for cleaning and shaping data using Power Query.

2. **Power BI Service**

An online software as a service (SaaS) service called the *Power BI service*.
- **Overview**: A cloud-based platform for sharing, collaborating, and managing Power BI reports and dashboards.
- **Features**:
    - **Publishing Reports**: Users can publish reports created in Power BI Desktop to the cloud for access by others.
    - **Dashboards**: Create dashboards that provide a single-page view of key metrics and KPIs.
    - **Collaboration**: Team members can comment, share, and collaborate on reports in real-time.

3. **Power BI Mobile**

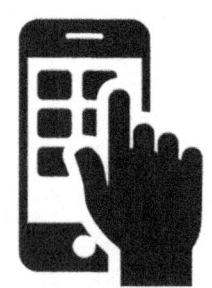

Power BI Mobile apps for Windows, iOS, and Android devices.
- **Overview**: Mobile applications for iOS and Android devices.
- **Features**:
    - **Access on the Go**: Users can view and interact with reports and dashboards from their mobile devices.
    - **Notifications**: Get alerts and notifications based on data changes or specified metrics.

4. **Power BI Gateway**

- **Overview**: A bridge that connects on-premises data sources to Power BI services.
- **Features**:
  - **Data Refresh**: Schedule regular updates for reports that pull data from on-premises sources.
  - **Live Queries**: Enable real-time access to data stored on local servers.

5. **Power BI Report Server**

Power BI Report Server, an on-premises report server where you can publish your Power BI reports, after creating them in Power BI Desktop.
- **Overview**: An on-premises report server for hosting Power BI reports.
- **Features**:
  - **Local Hosting**: Ideal for organizations that prefer to keep their data within their own infrastructure.
  - **Integration with Other Reports**: Supports traditional paginated reports and Power BI reports in a single server environment.

6. **Power BI Embedded**

- **Overview**: A service that allows developers to embed Power BI reports and dashboards into custom applications.
- **Features**:
  - **Custom Integration**: Users can incorporate rich analytics and reporting capabilities into their applications without requiring users to leave the app.
  - **User Management**: Provides APIs for managing user access and embedding reports securely.

7. **Data Connectors**

- **Overview**: Tools that facilitate connections to a wide range of data sources.
- **Features**:
  - **Diverse Sources**: Connect to databases (like SQL Server), online services (like Salesforce), and flat files (like Excel and CSV).
  - **Ease of Use**: Streamlined connection process for users to import data easily.

8. **Power Query**

- **Overview**: A data connection technology integrated within Power BI.
- **Features**:
  - **Data Transformation**: Allows users to clean, reshape, and transform data before loading it into Power BI for analysis.
  - **User-Friendly Interface**: Offers a GUI for performing data manipulation without needing complex coding.

9. **DAX (Data Analysis Expressions)**
   - **Overview**: A formula language used in Power BI for creating calculated columns, measures, and tables.
   - **Features**:
     - **Powerful Calculations**: Enables users to perform advanced calculations on data.
     - **Similar to Excel**: Familiarity for users who have experience with Excel formulas, making it easier to learn.

10. **Power BI Report Builder**: For creating paginated reports to share in the Power BI service.

These products components work together to provide a comprehensive platform for data analysis, reporting, and business intelligence, enabling users to make informed decisions based on their data.

2.7 Power BI Desktop

Power BI Desktop is a free application you install on your local computer that lets you connect to, transform, and visualize your data. With Power BI Desktop, you can connect to multiple different sources of data, and combine them (often called *modeling*) into a data model. This data model lets you build visuals, and collections of visuals you can share as reports, with other people inside your organization. Most users who work on business intelligence projects use Power BI Desktop to create reports, and then use the *Power BI service* to share their reports with others.

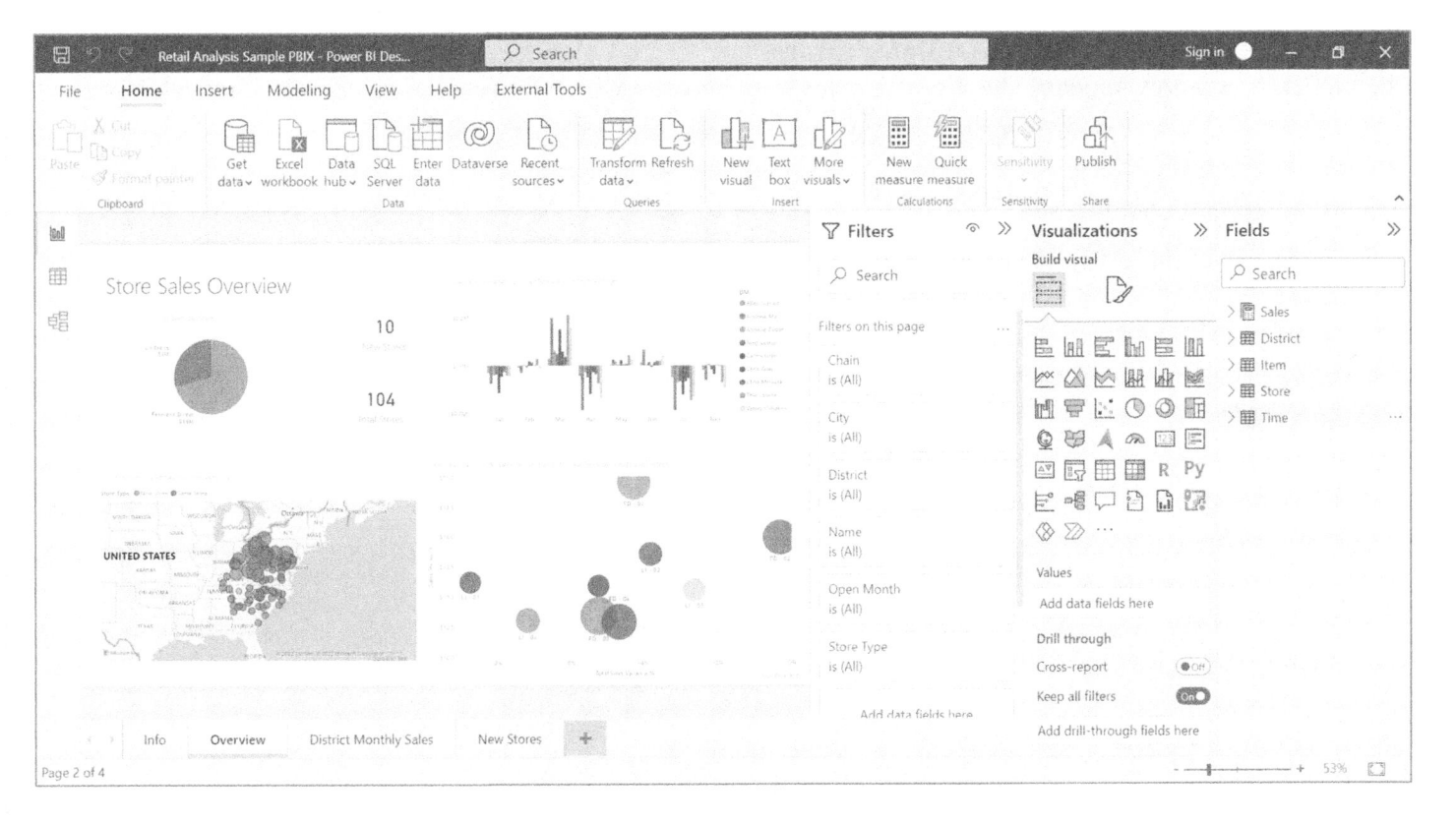

Views in Power BI Desktop

There are three views available in Power BI Desktop, which you select on the left side of the canvas. The views, shown in the order they appear, are as follows:
- **Report**: You create reports and visuals, where most of your creation time is spent.
- **Data**: You see the tables, measures, and other data used in the data model associated with your report, and transform the data for best use in the report's model.
- **Model**: You see and manage the relationships among tables in your data model.

The following image shows the three views, as displayed along the left side of the canvas:

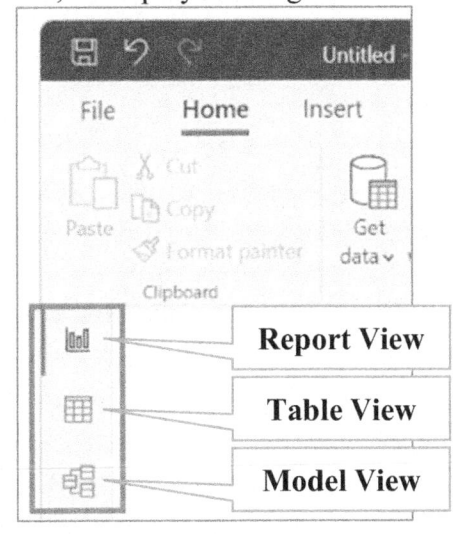

Connect to Data Sources

To get started with Power BI Desktop, the first step is to connect to data. There are many different data sources you can connect to from Power BI Desktop.
To connect to data:

1. From the **Home** ribbon, select **Get Data** > **More**.
The **Get Data** window appears, showing the many categories to which Power BI Desktop can connect.

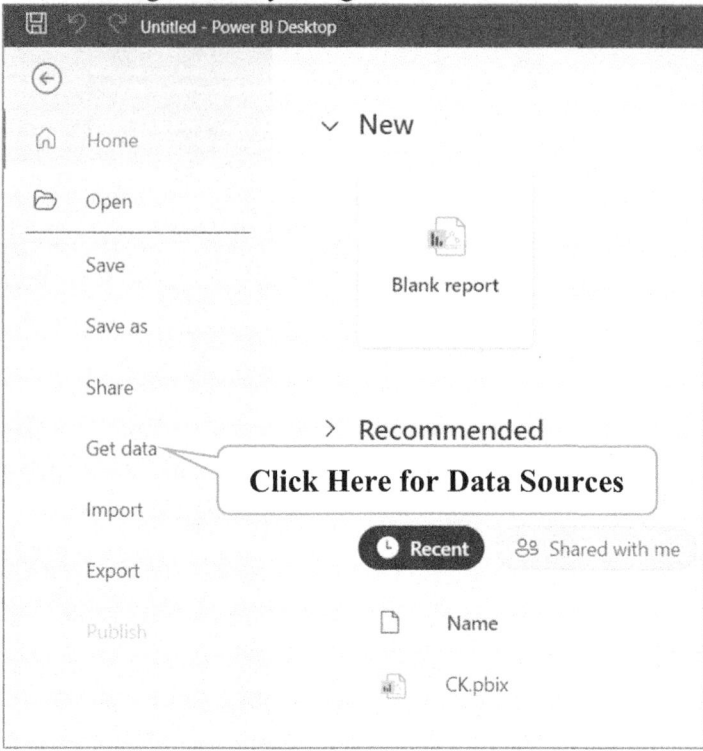

2. When you select a data type, you're prompted for information, such as the URL and credentials, necessary for Power BI Desktop to connect to the data source on your behalf.
From Files like Excel files, CSV File:

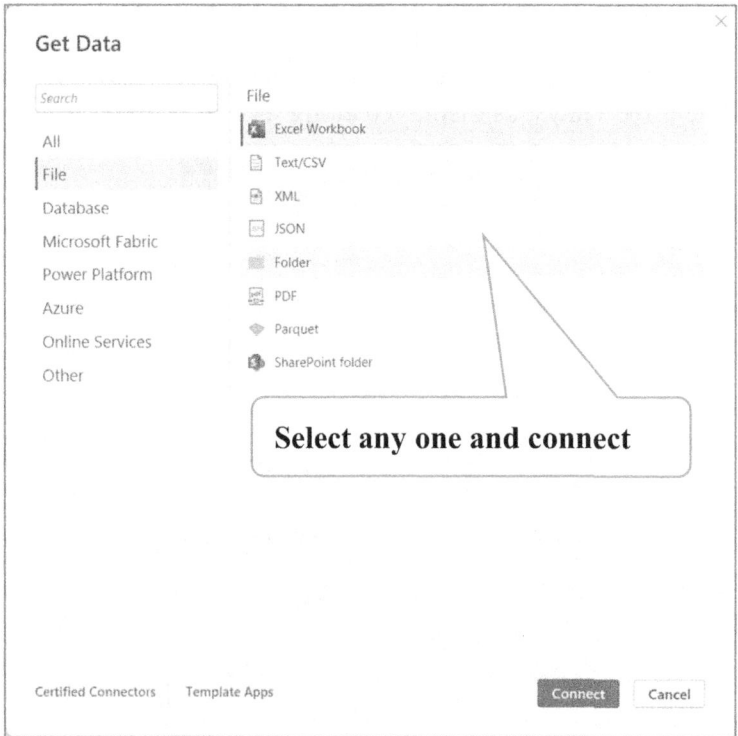

From Databases like SQL server, and Oracle:

Get Data — Database

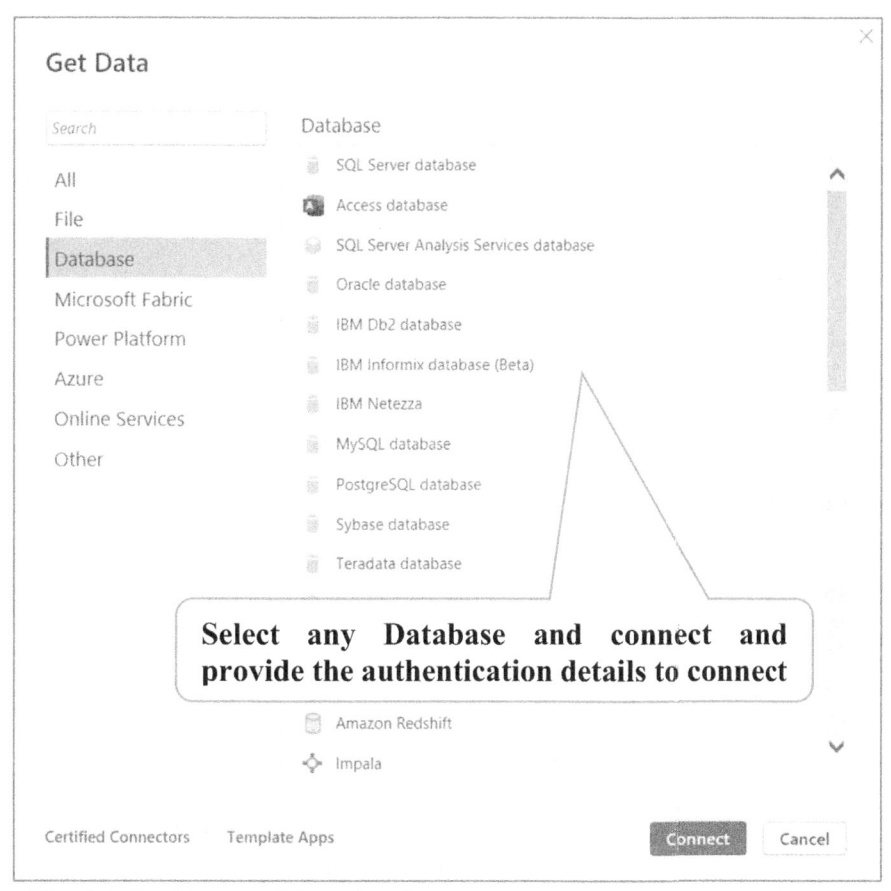

Search
- All
- File
- **Database**
- Microsoft Fabric
- Power Platform
- Azure
- Online Services
- Other

Database:
- SQL Server database
- Access database
- SQL Server Analysis Services database
- Oracle database
- IBM Db2 database
- IBM Informix database (Beta)
- IBM Netezza
- MySQL database
- PostgreSQL database
- Sybase database
- Teradata database
- Amazon Redshift
- Impala

Select any Database and connect and provide the authentication details to connect

Certified Connectors | Template Apps | Connect | Cancel

From online services like Linked In, and Facebook:

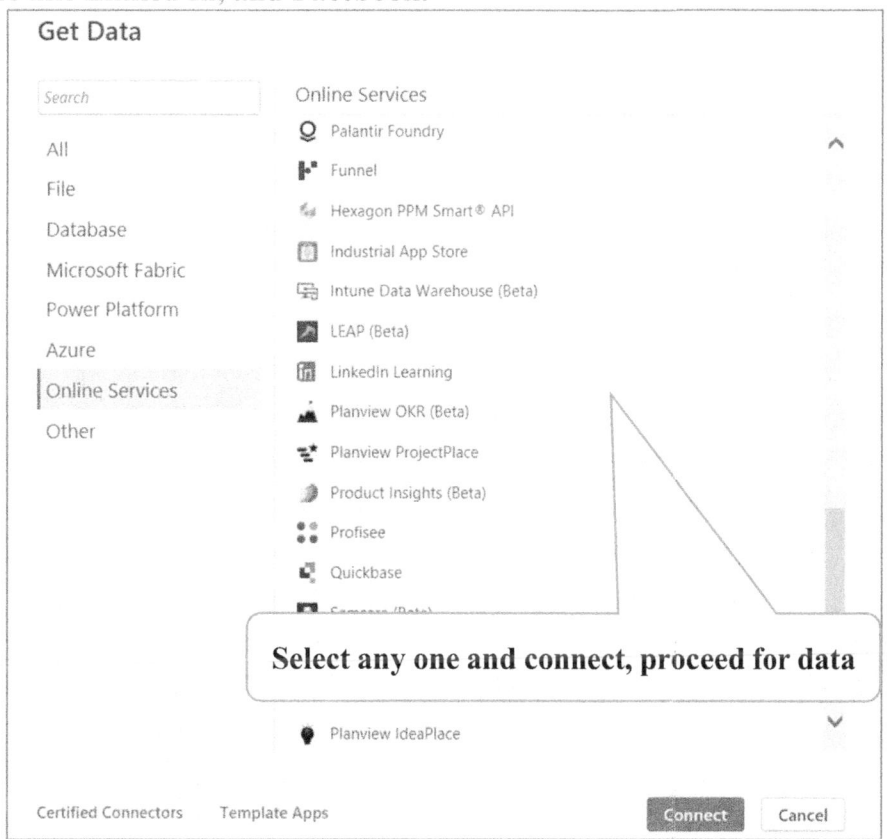

Get Data — Online Services

Search
- All
- File
- Database
- Microsoft Fabric
- Power Platform
- Azure
- **Online Services**
- Other

Online Services:
- Palantir Foundry
- Funnel
- Hexagon PPM Smart® API
- Industrial App Store
- Intune Data Warehouse (Beta)
- LEAP (Beta)
- LinkedIn Learning
- Planview OKR (Beta)
- Planview ProjectPlace
- Product Insights (Beta)
- Profisee
- Quickbase
- Planview IdeaPlace

Select any one and connect, proceed for data

Certified Connectors | Template Apps | Connect | Cancel

From online sources like Web, and Spark:

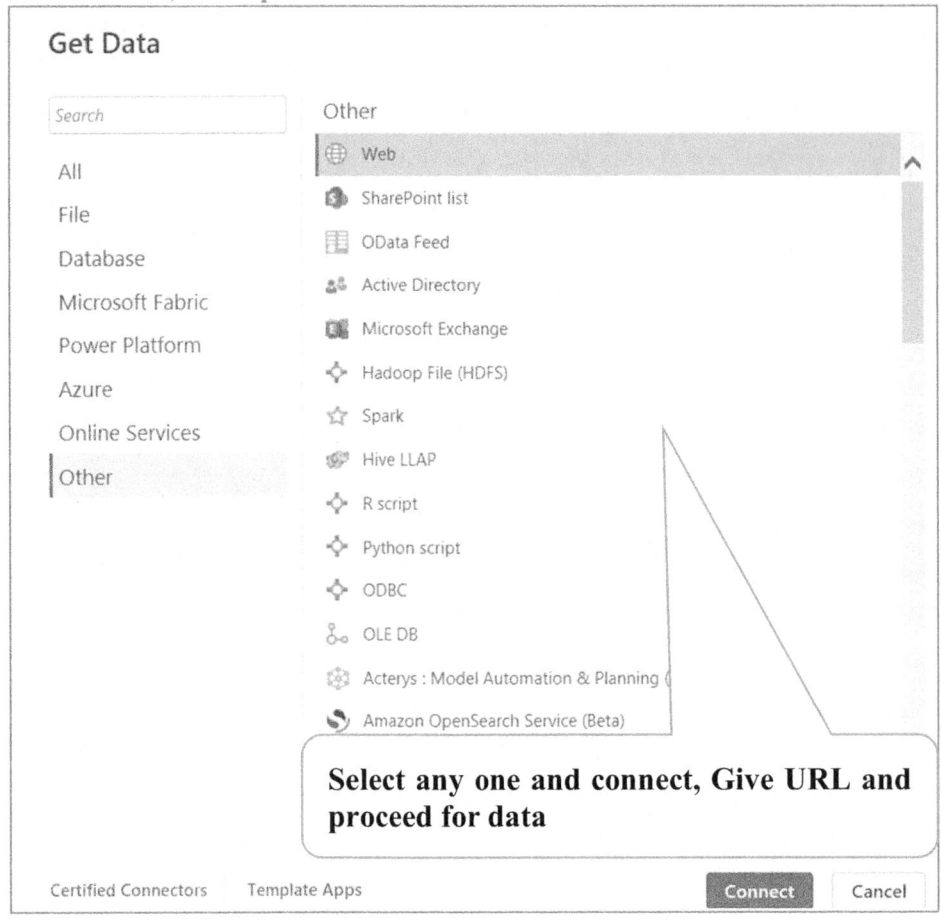

Get Data

	Other
All	🌐 Web
File	👥 SharePoint list
Database	📊 OData Feed
Microsoft Fabric	👥 Active Directory
Power Platform	📧 Microsoft Exchange
Azure	◆ Hadoop File (HDFS)
Online Services	☆ Spark
Other	🐝 Hive LLAP
	◆ R script
	◆ Python script
	◆ ODBC
	🔗 OLE DB
	🎲 Acterys : Model Automation & Planning
	🔍 Amazon OpenSearch Service (Beta)

Select any one and connect, Give URL and proceed for data

Certified Connectors   Template Apps   Connect   Cancel

From Azure databases like Azure SQL, Azure Cost Management:

Select any Azure Database and connect and provide the authentication details to connect

Create Visuals

After you have a data model, you can drag *fields* onto the report canvas to create *visuals*. A visual is a graphic representation of the data in your model. There are many different types of visuals to choose from in Power BI Desktop. The following visual shows a simple column chart.

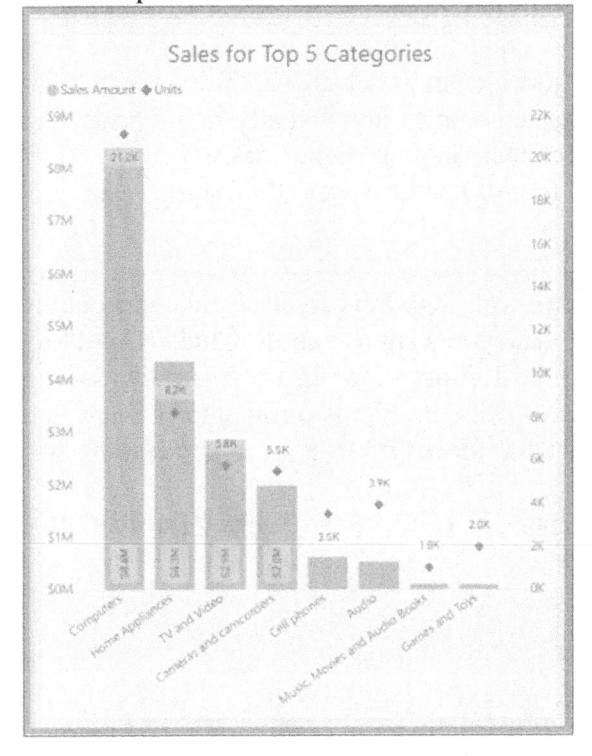

To create or change a visual:
- From the **Visualizations** pane, select the **Build visual** icon.

Create Reports

More often, you'll want to create a collection of visuals that show various aspects of the data you've used to create your model in Power BI Desktop. A collection of visuals, in one Power BI Desktop file, is called a *report*. A report can have one or more pages, just like an Excel file can have one or more worksheets.

With Power BI Desktop you can create complex and visually rich reports, using data from multiple sources, all in one report that you can share with others in your organization.

In the following image, you see the first page of a Power BI Desktop report, named **Overview**, as seen on the tab near the bottom of the image.

Steps to create reports
1. Get Data from the data source (Excel, SQL Server, etc.) and connect to it
2. Load data: Select the tables or data you want to import. Click **"Load"** to bring the data into Power BI.
3. Design the Report: Switch to the **Report** view. In the **Visualizations pane**, select different visual types (e.g., bar chart, table).Drag fields from the **Fields pane** onto the canvas to populate your visuals.
4. Format Visuals:Click on a visual to format it using the **Format pane**.Adjust colors, labels, titles, and other settings to enhance appearance
5. Save and Publish:Save your report file (File > Save).Click **"Publish"** to upload your report to the Power BI Service.

Share Reports

After a report is ready to share with others, you can *publish* the report to the Power BI service, and make it available to anyone in your organization who has a Power BI license.

To publish a Power BI Desktop report:

1. Select **Publish** from the **Home** ribbon.

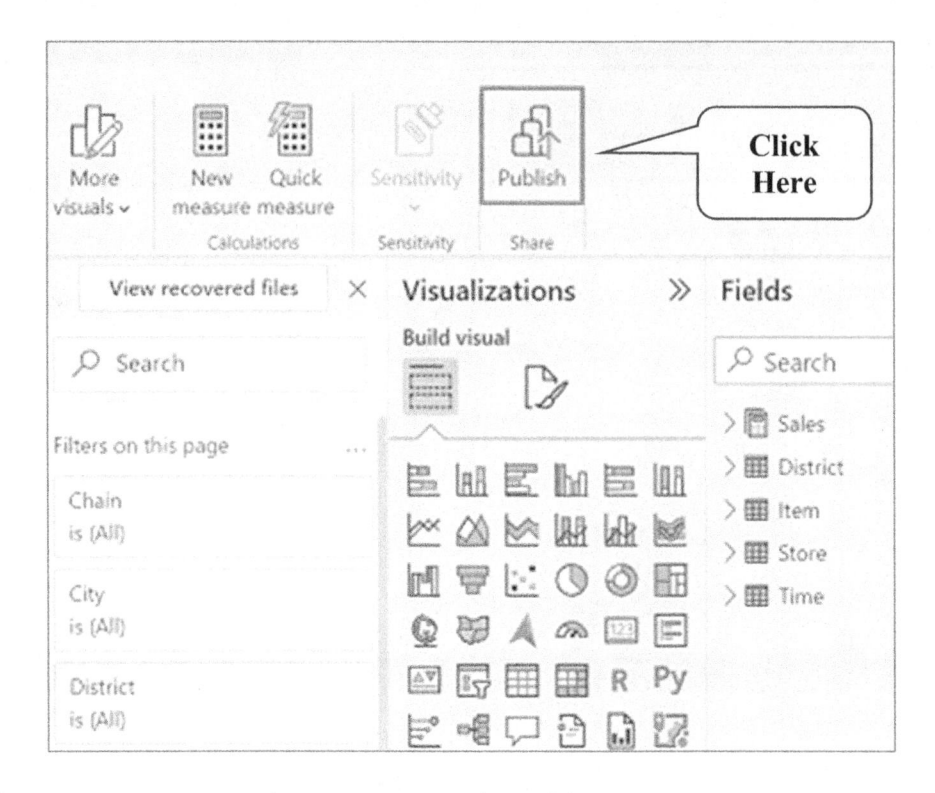

1. Power BI Desktop connects you to the Power BI service with your Power BI account.
2. You're prompted to select where in the Power BI service you'd like to share the report. For example, your workspace, a team workspace, or some other location in the Power BI service.

You must have a Power BI license to share reports to the Power BI service.

2.8 Power BI Visual Elements

Area charts: Basic (Layered) and Stacked:

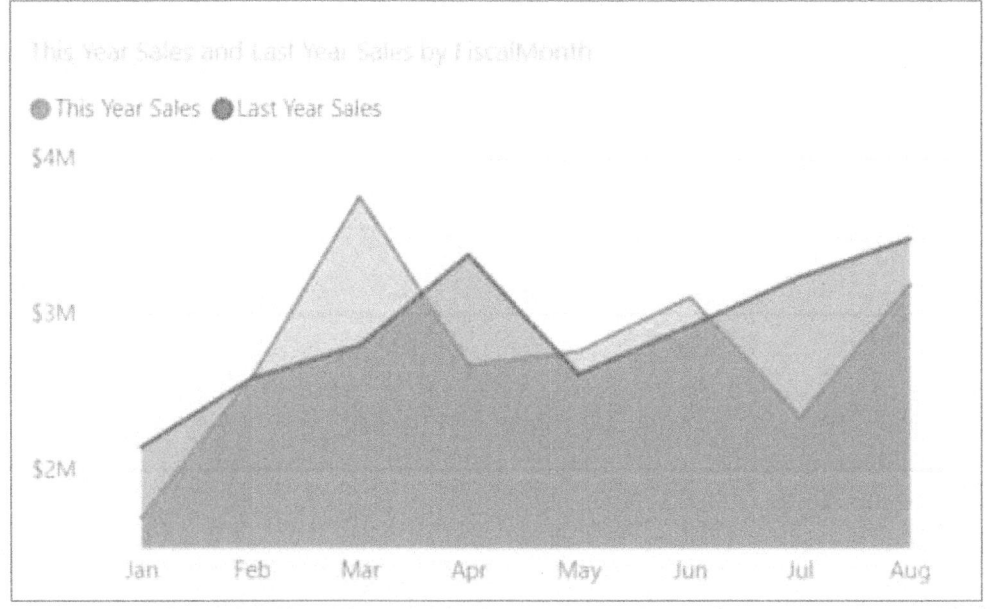

The basic area chart is based on the line chart with the area between the axis and line filled in. Area charts emphasize the magnitude of change over time, and can be used to draw attention to the total value across a trend. For example, data that represents profit over time can be plotted in an area chart to emphasize the total profit. On the other hand, stacked area charts display the cumulative total of multiple data series stacked on top of each other, showing how each series contributes to the total.

Bar and column charts:

Bar and column charts are two of the most commonly used chart types in Power BI. Both charts use rectangular bars to display data, with the length of the bar representing the value of the data. The main difference between the two is the orientation of the bars:
Bar charts: Bars are displayed horizontally across the x-axis.
Column charts: Bars are displayed vertically on the y-axis.

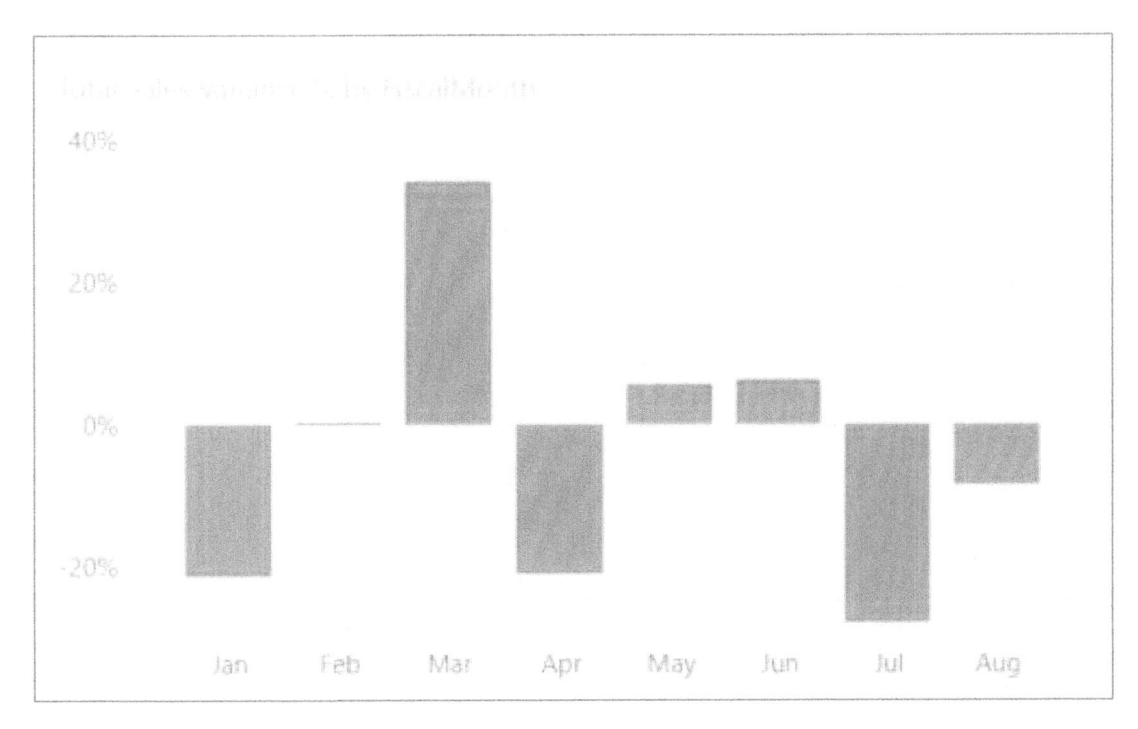

Bar charts are the standard for looking at a specific value across different categories. They are a very simple and uncomplicated way to show comparison or ranking in a range of values. The bars in a bar chart are displayed horizontally across the axis and in a column chart they are displayed vertically

Cards:
Multi row

> **030-Kids**
> **$5.30**
> Average Unit Price

Multi row cards display one or more data points, one per row.
Single number

> **104**
> Total Stores

Single number cards display a single fact, a single data point. Sometimes a single number is the most important thing you want to track in your Power BI dashboard or report, such as total sales, market share year over year, or total opportunities.

Combo charts

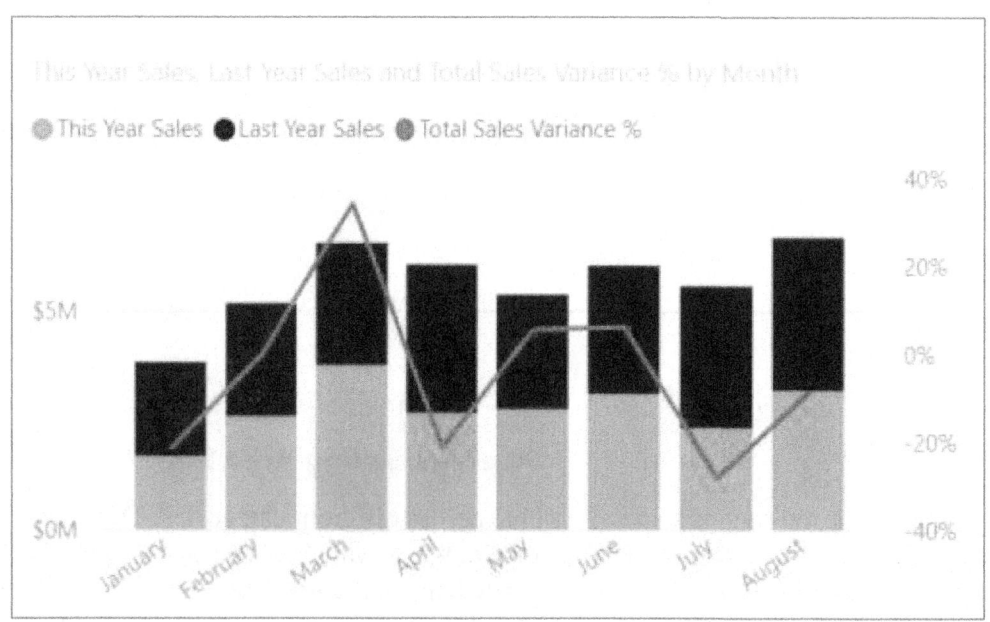

A combo chart combines a column chart and a line chart. Combining the two charts into one lets you make a quicker comparison of the data. Combo charts can have one or two Y axes, so be sure to look closely.
Combo charts are a great choice:

- When you have a line chart and a column chart with the same X axis.
- To compare multiple measures with different value ranges.
- To illustrate the correlation between two measures in one visual.
- To check whether one measure meets the target, which is defined by another measure.
- To conserve canvas space.

Decomposition tree:

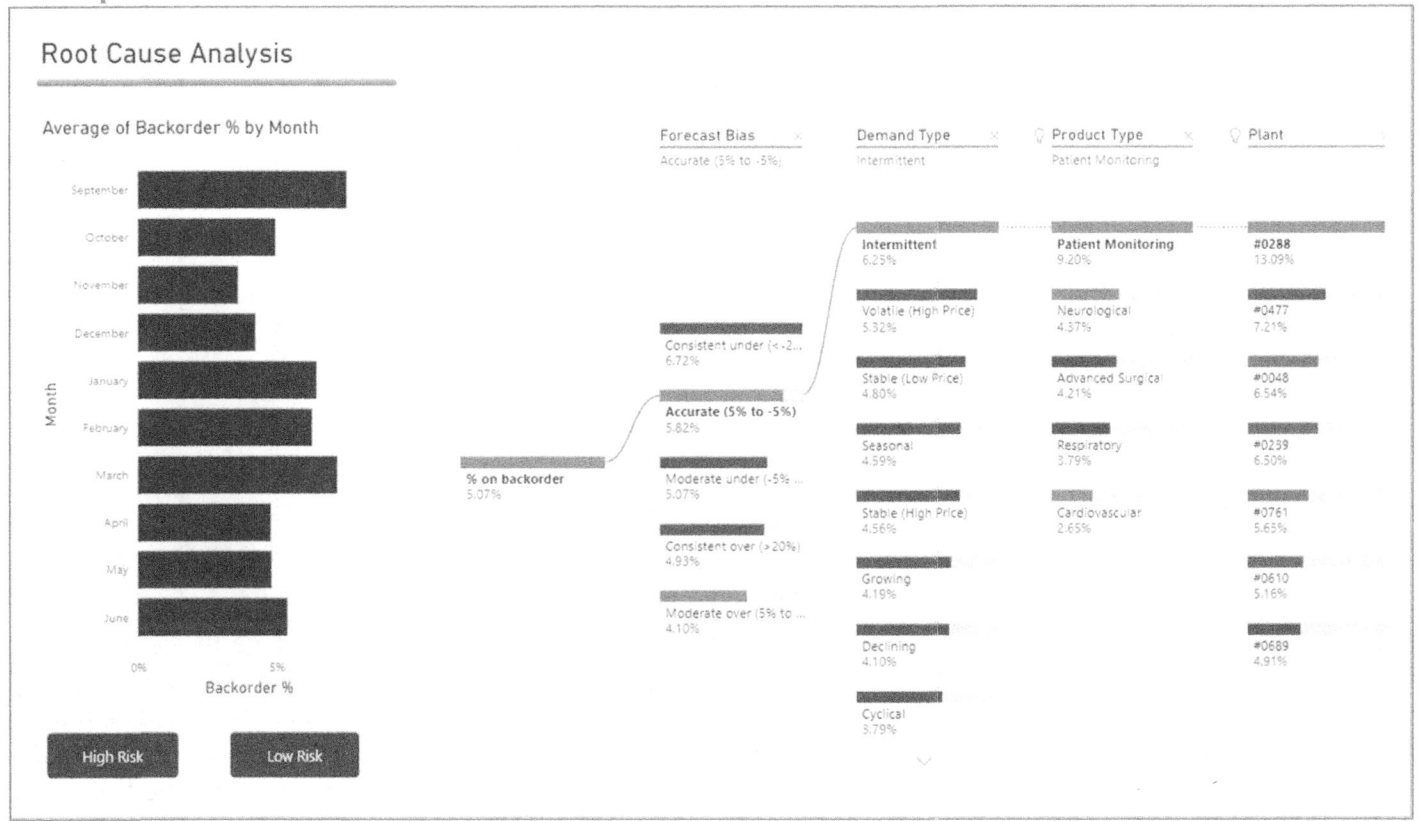

The decomposition tree visual lets you visualize data across multiple dimensions. It automatically aggregates data and enables drilling down into your dimensions in any order. It is also an artificial intelligence (AI) visualization, so you can ask it to find the next dimension to drill down into based on certain criteria. This capability makes it a valuable tool for ad hoc exploration and conducting root cause analysis.

Doughnut charts:

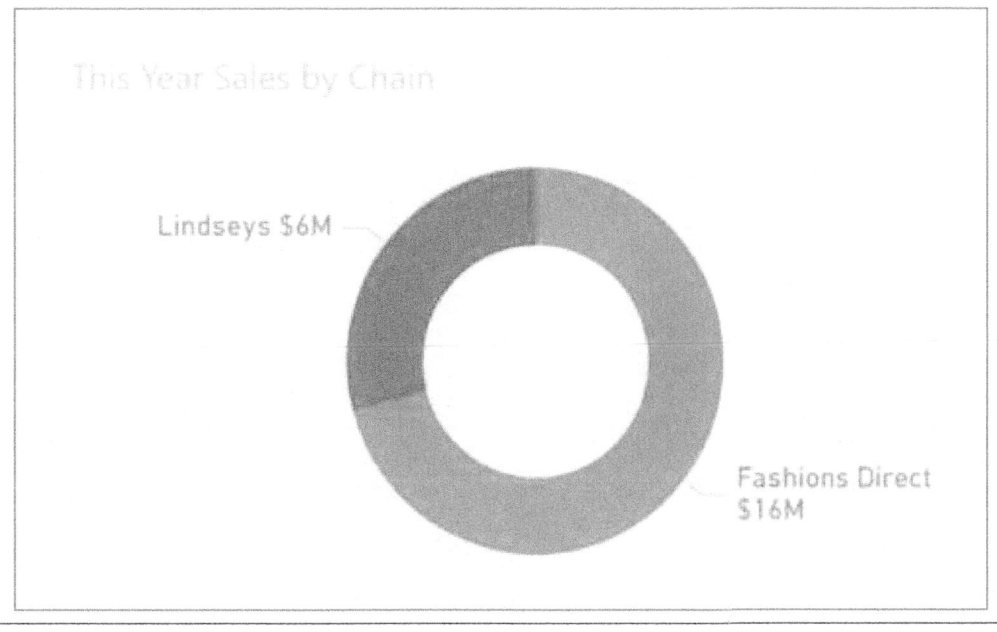

Doughnut charts are similar to pie charts. They show the relationship of parts to a whole. The only difference is that the center is blank and allows space for a label or icon.

Funnel charts:

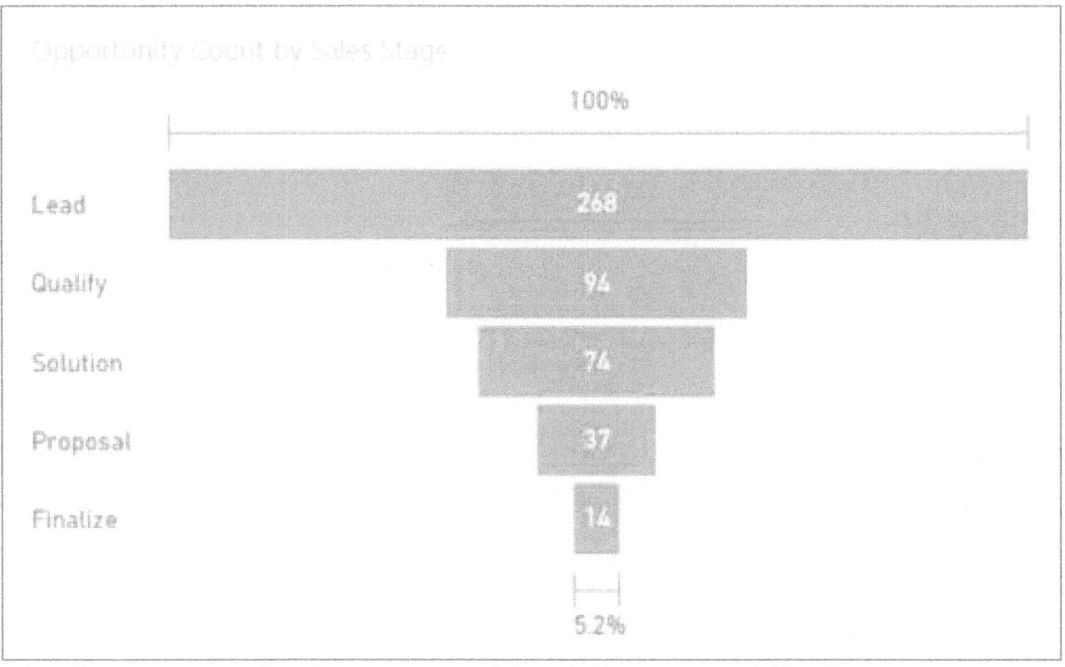

Funnels help visualize a process that has stages, and items flow sequentially from one stage to the next. One example is a sales process that starts with leads and ends with purchase fulfillment.

For example, a sales funnel that tracks customers through stages: Lead > Qualified Lead > Prospect > Contract > Close. At a glance, the shape of the funnel conveys the health of the process you're tracking. Each funnel stage represents a percentage of the total. So, in most cases, a funnel chart is shaped like a funnel -- with the first stage being the largest, and each subsequent stage smaller than its predecessor. A pear-shaped funnel is also useful -- it can identify a problem in the process. But typically, the first stage, the "intake" stage, is the largest.

Gauge charts:

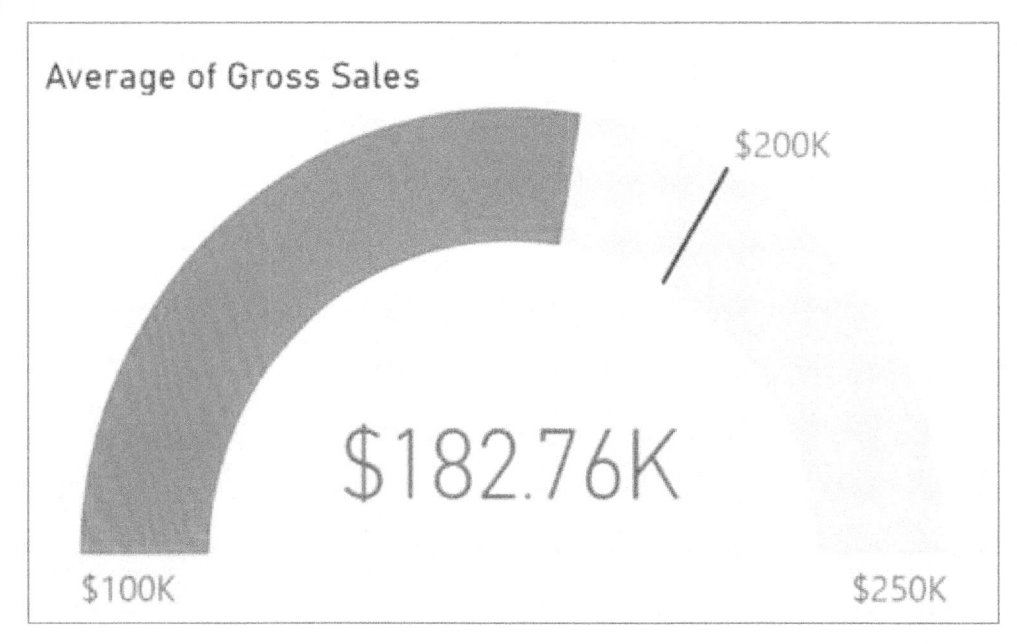

A radial gauge chart has a circular arc and displays a single value that measures progress toward a goal. The goal, or target value, is represented by the line (needle). Progress toward that goal is represented by the shading. And the value that represents that progress is shown in bold inside the arc. All possible values are spread evenly along the arc, from the minimum (left-most value) to the maximum (right-most value).

In the example, we are a car retailer, tracking our Sales team's average sales per month. Our goal is 200,000 and represented by the location of the needle. The minimum possible average sales is 100,000 and we set the maximum as 250,000. The blue shading shows that we're currently averaging approximately $180,000 this month. Luckily, we still have another week to reach our goal.

Radial gauges are a great choice to:
- Show progress toward a goal.
- Represent a percentile measure, like a KPI.
- Show the health of a single measure.
- Display information that can be quickly scanned and understood.

Key influencers chart:

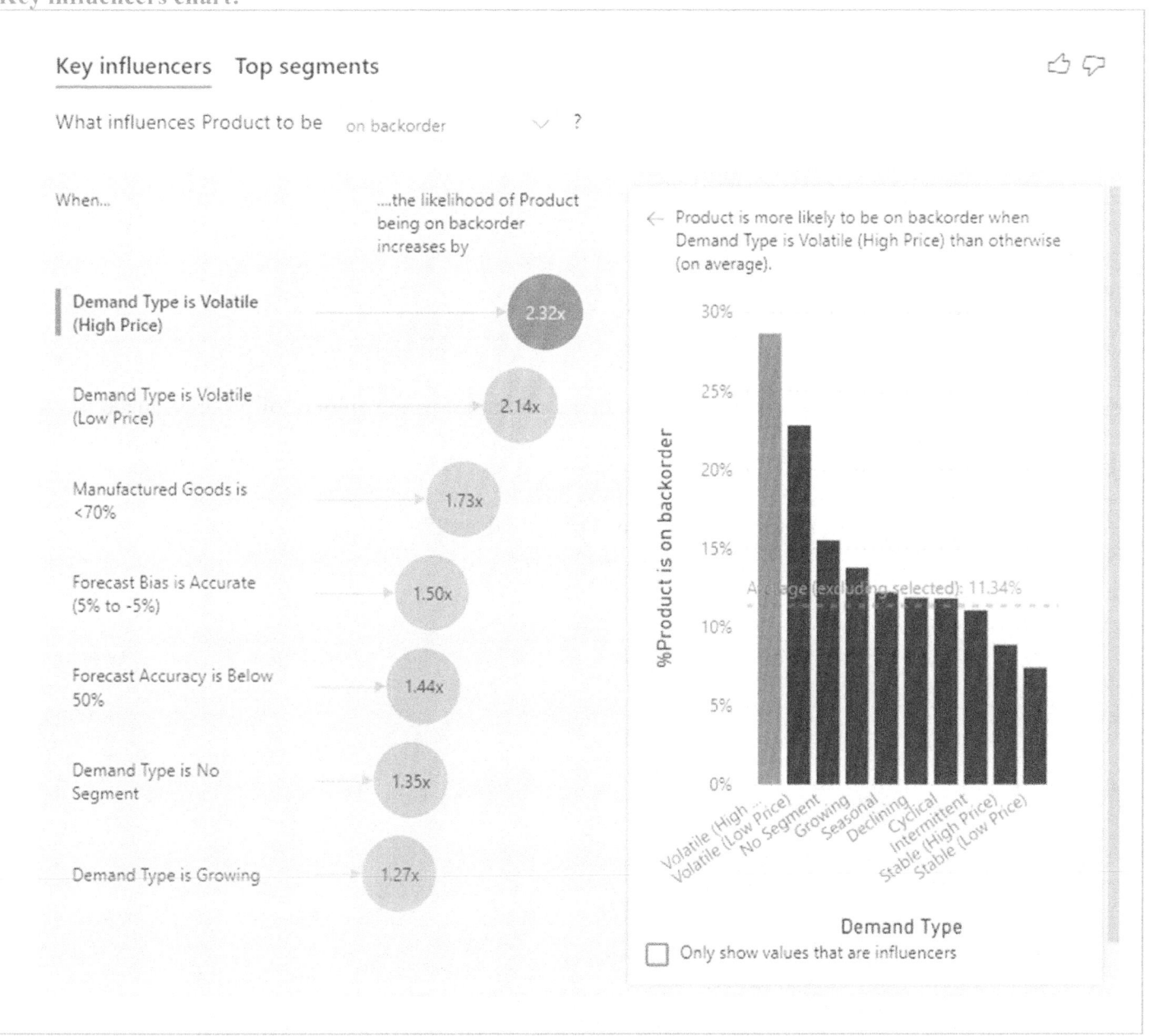

A key influencer chart displays the major contributors to a selected result or value.

Key influencers are a great choice to help you understand the factors that influence a key metric. For example, *what influences customers to place a second order* or *why were sales so high last June*.

KPIs:

$482,537
Goal: $595,092 (-18.91%)

Total Units This Year and Total Units Last Year by Month

A Key Performance Indicator (KPI) is a visual cue that communicates the amount of progress made toward a measurable goal.

KPIs are a great choice:
- To measure progress (what am I ahead or behind on?).
- To measure distance to a metric (how far ahead or behind am I?)

Line charts:

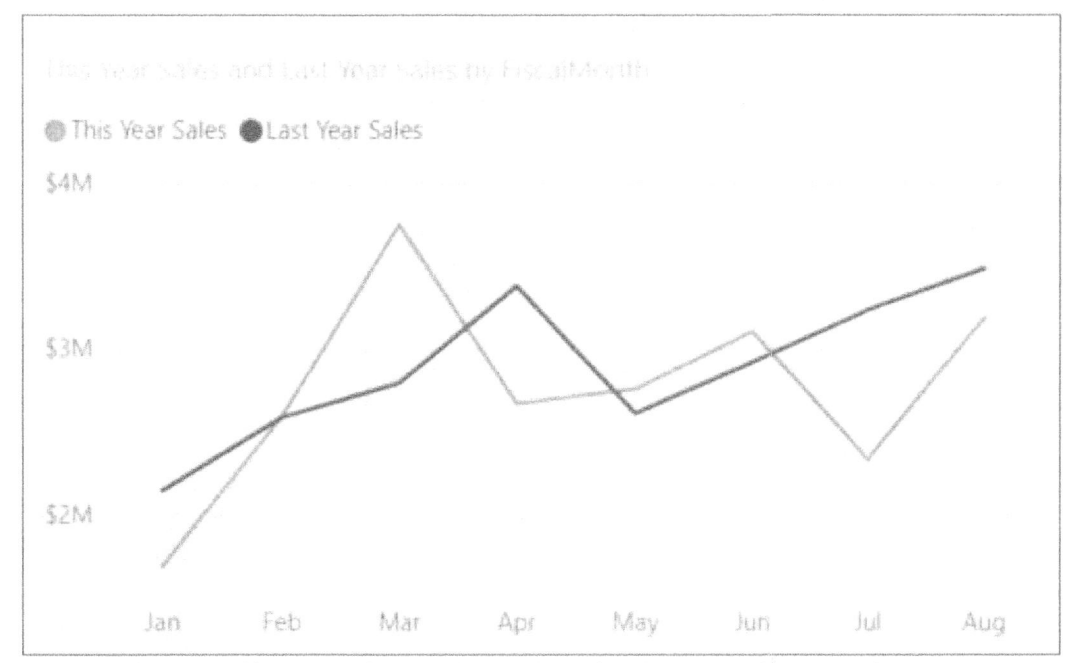

Line charts emphasize the overall shape of an entire series of values, usually over time.

Maps:
Basic map

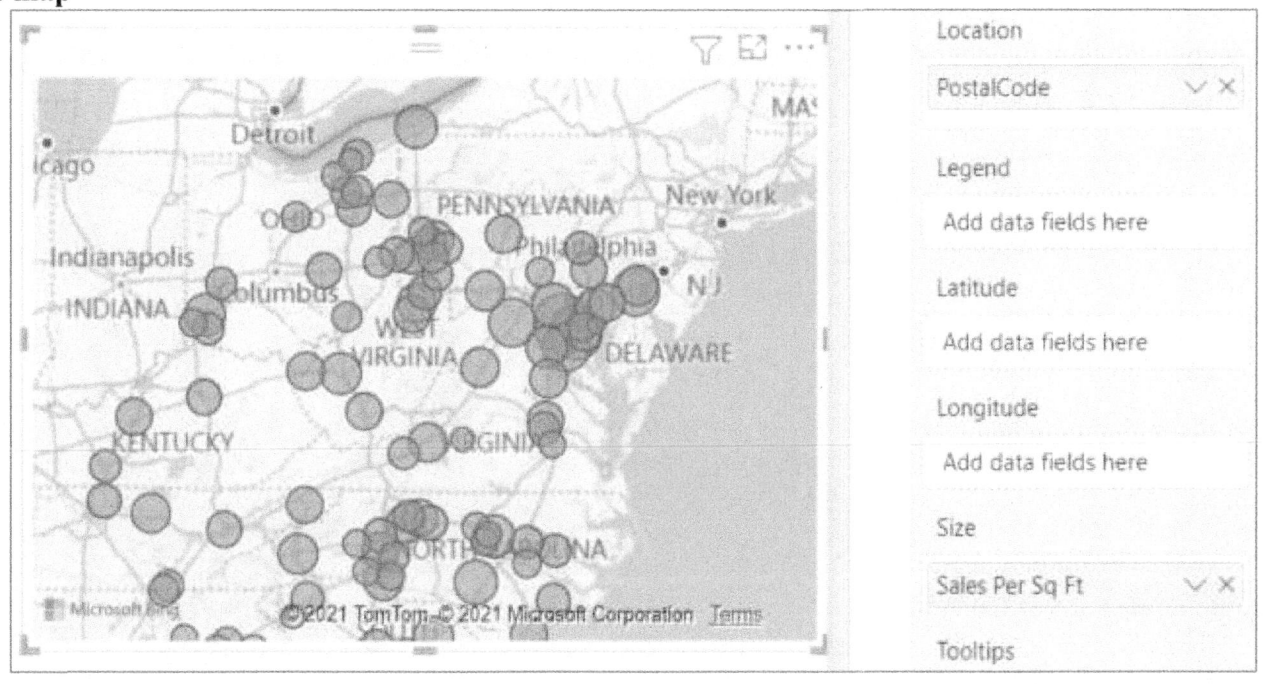

Use a basic map to associate both categorical and quantitative information with spatial locations. The Power BI service and Power BI Desktop send Bing the geo data it needs to create the map visualization. This data may include the data in the **Location**, **Latitude**, and **Longitude** buckets of the visual's field well

ArcGIS map

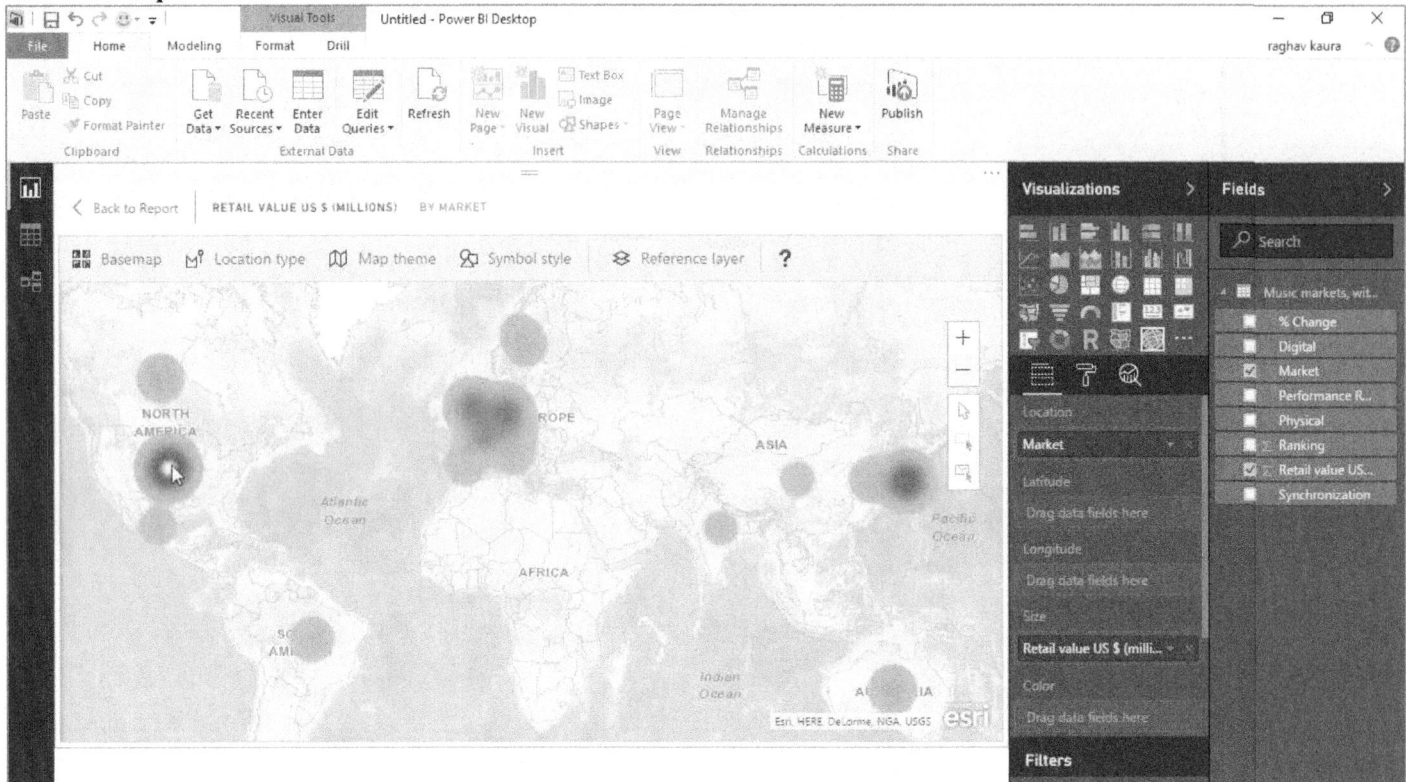

The combination of ArcGIS maps and Power BI takes mapping beyond the presentation of points on a map to a whole new level. The available options for base maps, location types, themes, symbol styles, and reference layers creates gorgeous informative map visuals. The combination of authoritative data layers (such as census data) on a map with spatial analysis conveys a deeper understanding of the data in your visual.

Azure map

31

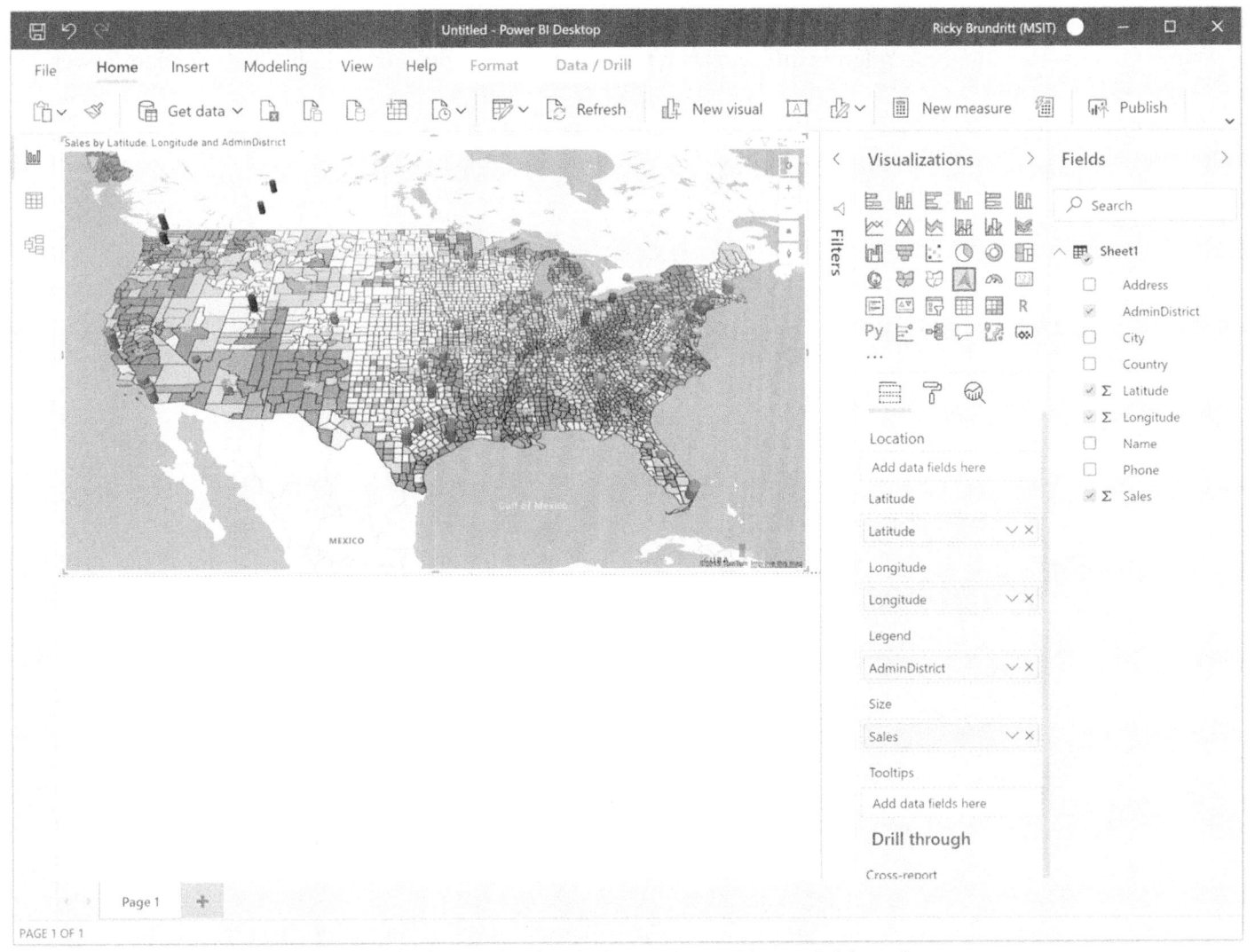

Used to associate both categorical and quantitative information with spatial locations.
Filled map (Choropleth)

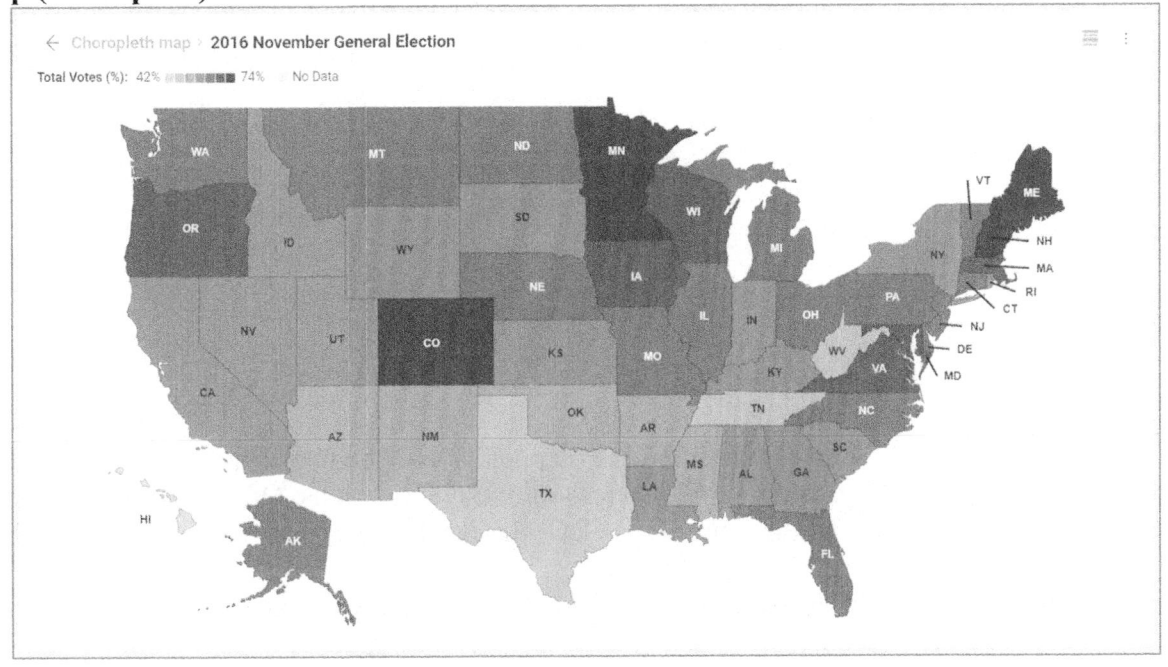

A filled map uses shading or tinting or patterns to display how a value differs in proportion across a geography or region. Quickly display these relative differences with shading that ranges from light (less-frequent/lower) to dark (more-frequent/more).
The more intense the color, the larger the value.

Shape map

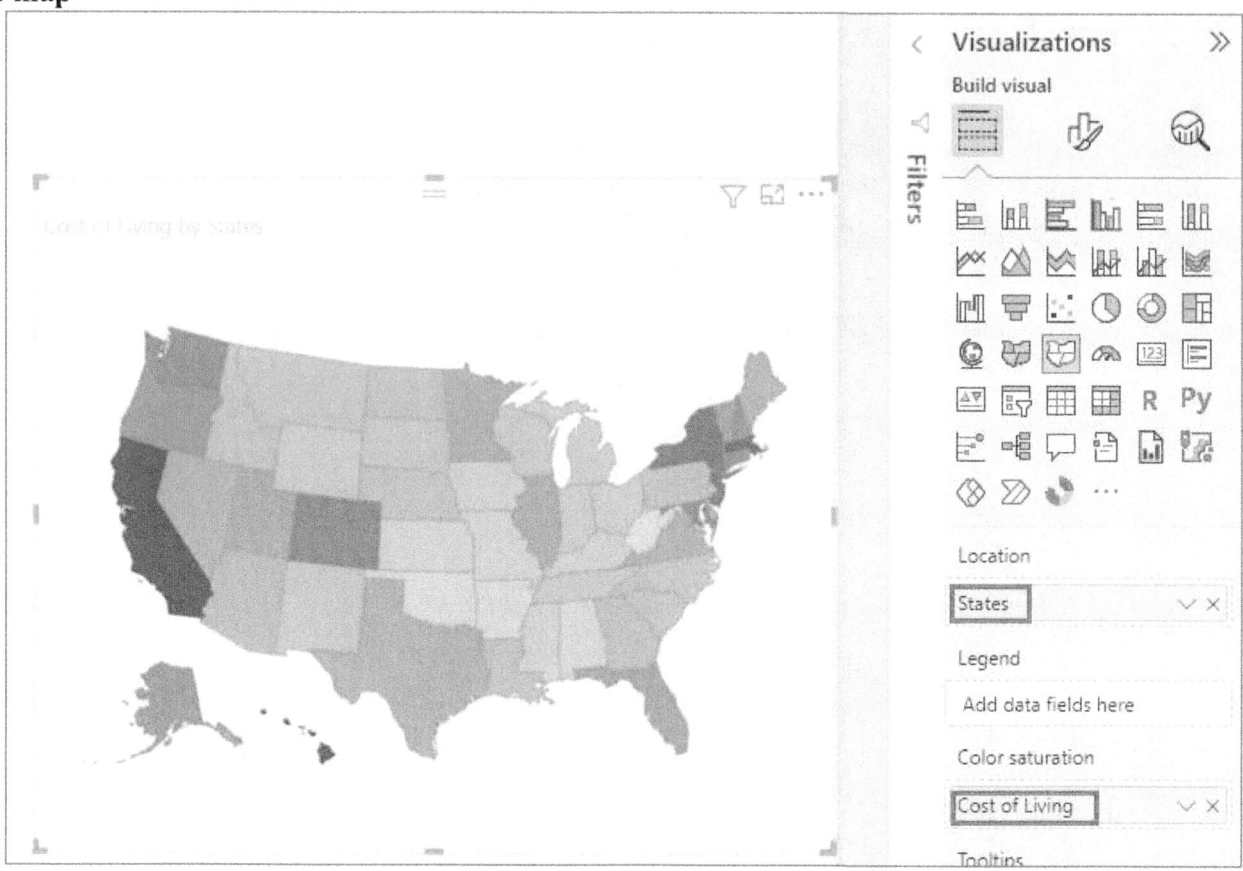

Shape maps compare regions on a map using color. A shape map can't show precise geographical locations of data points on a map. Instead, its main purpose is to show relative comparisons of regions on a map by coloring them differently.

Matrix:

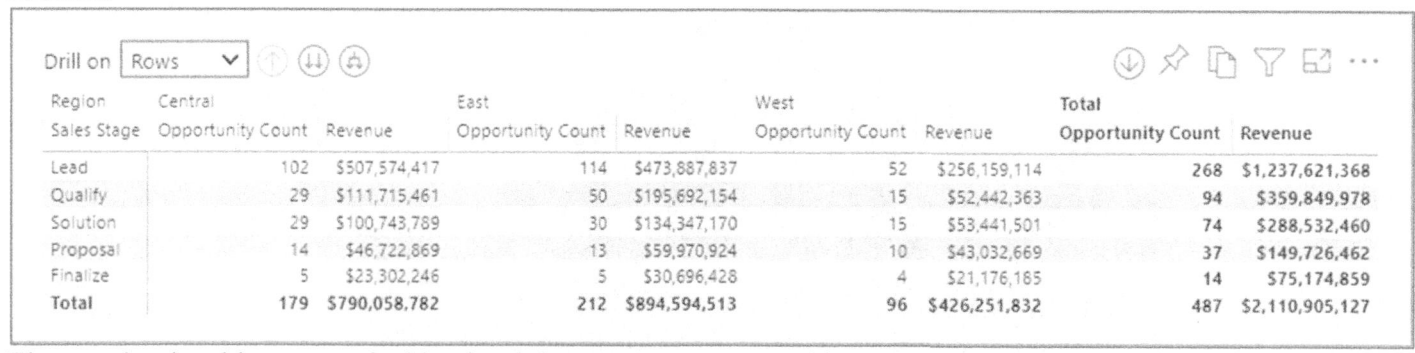

Region	Central		East		West		Total	
Sales Stage	Opportunity Count	Revenue	Opportunity Count	Revenue	Opportunity Count	Revenue	Opportunity Count	Revenue
Lead	102	$507,574,417	114	$473,887,837	52	$256,159,114	268	$1,237,621,368
Qualify	29	$111,715,461	50	$195,692,154	15	$52,442,363	94	$359,849,978
Solution	29	$100,743,789	30	$134,347,170	15	$53,441,501	74	$288,532,460
Proposal	14	$46,722,869	13	$59,970,924	10	$43,032,669	37	$149,726,462
Finalize	5	$23,302,246	5	$30,696,428	4	$21,176,185	14	$75,174,859
Total	179	$790,058,782	212	$894,594,513	96	$426,251,832	487	$2,110,905,127

The matrix visual is a type of table visual that supports a stepped layout. A table supports two dimensions, but a matrix makes it easier to display data meaningfully across multiple dimensions. Often, report designers include matrixes in reports and dashboards to allow users to select one or more element (rows, columns, cells) in the matrix to cross-highlight other visuals on a report page.
The matrix automatically aggregates the data and enables drilling down into the data.

Pie charts:

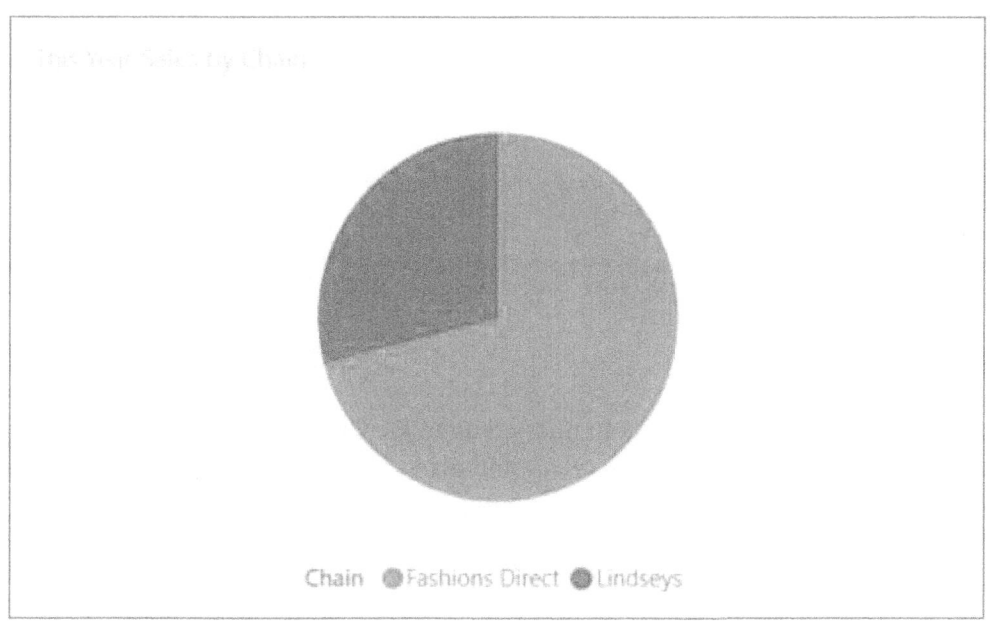

pie charts show the relationship of parts to a whole.

Power Apps visual:

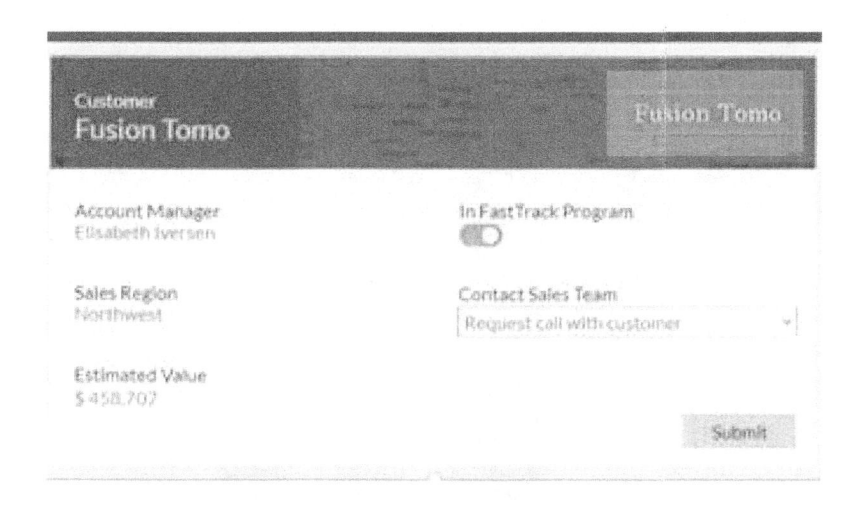

Report designers can create a Power App and embed it into a Power BI report as a visual. Consumers can interact with that visual within the Power BI report.

Q&A visual:

The Q&A visual provides users with a text box to query data in Power BI reports. Users can use natural language to query data, and the Q&A visual interprets the query and provides an appropriate visualization.

For example, if a user asks a question like "What were the product sales in 2019?" the Q&A visual queries the relevant data and create an appropriate visualization to display the results. This visualization can be in many different formats, such as a chart or a table.

Similar to the [Q&A experience on dashboards](#), the Q&A visual lets you ask questions about your data using natural language.

R script visuals:

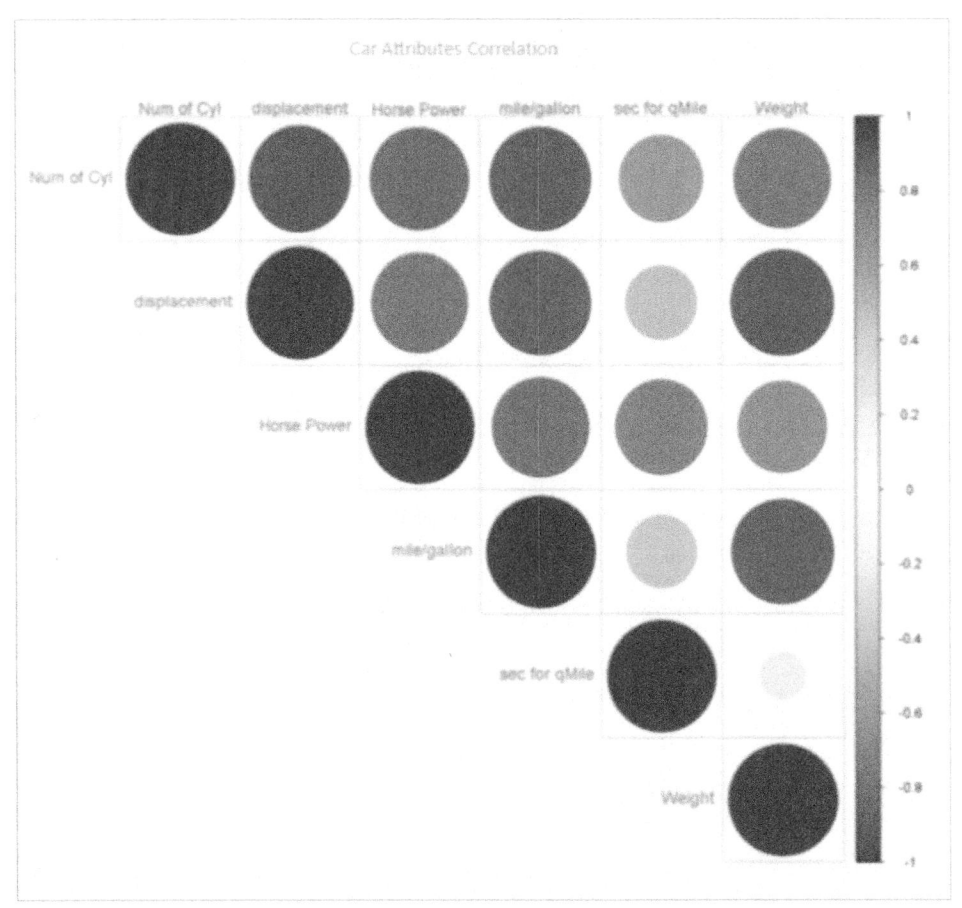

Visuals created with R scripts, commonly called *R visuals*, can present advanced data shaping and analytics such as forecasting, using the rich analytics and visualization power of R. R visuals can be created in Power BI Desktop and published to the Power BI service.

Ribbon chart:

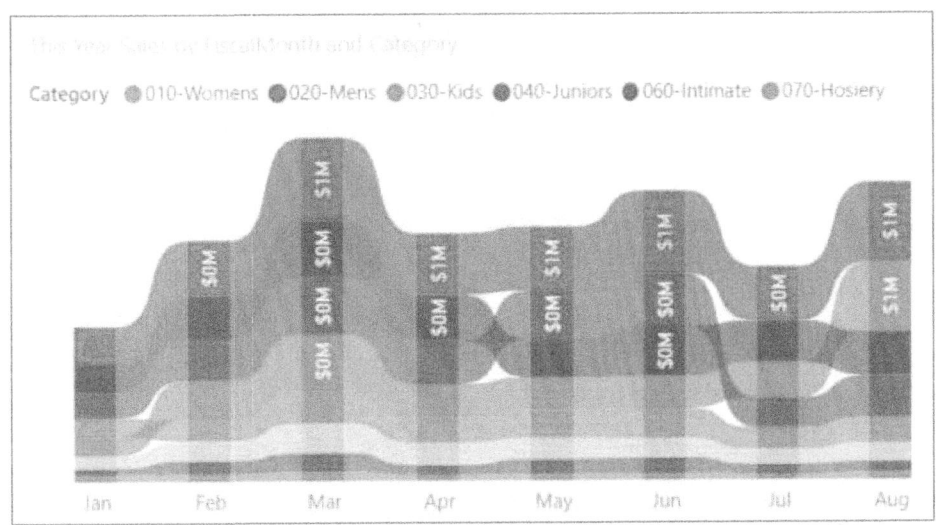

Ribbon charts show which data category has the highest rank (largest value). Ribbon charts are effective at showing rank change, with the highest range (value) always displayed on top for each time period.

Scatter:

Scatter, bubble, and dot plot chart

A scatter chart always has two value axes to show one set of numerical data along a horizontal axis and another set of numerical values along a vertical axis. The chart displays points at the intersection of an x and y numerical value, combining these values into single data points. These data points might be distributed evenly or unevenly across the horizontal axis, depending on the data.

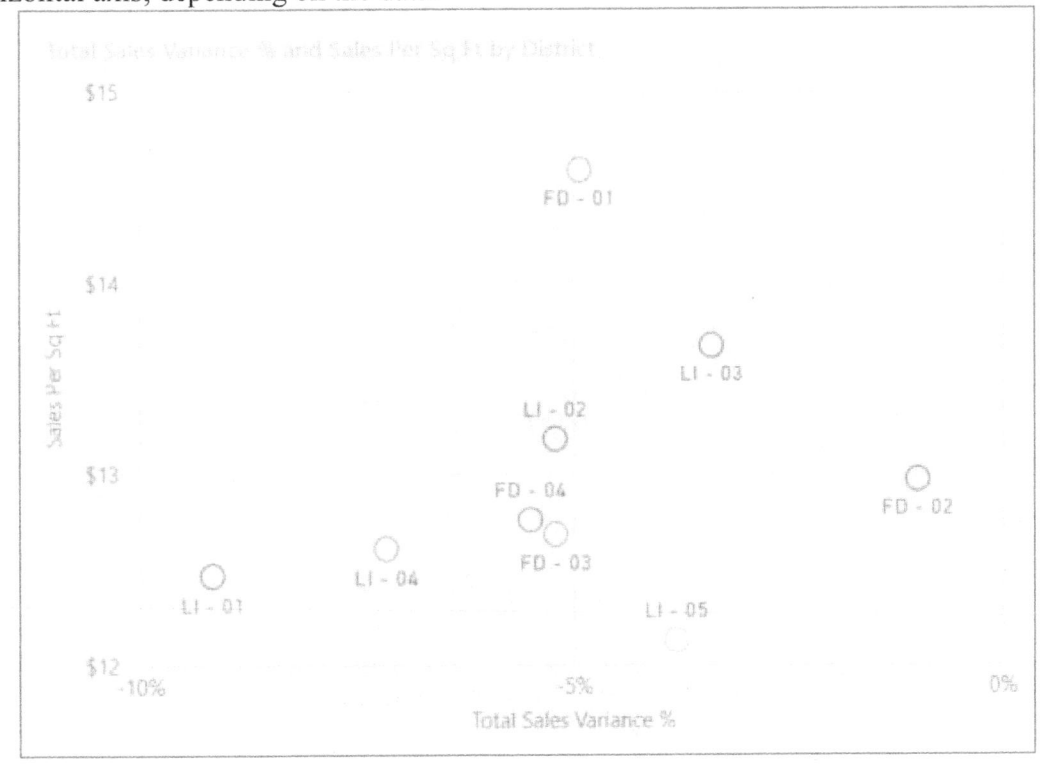

A bubble chart replaces data points with bubbles, with the bubble size representing an additional dimension of the data.

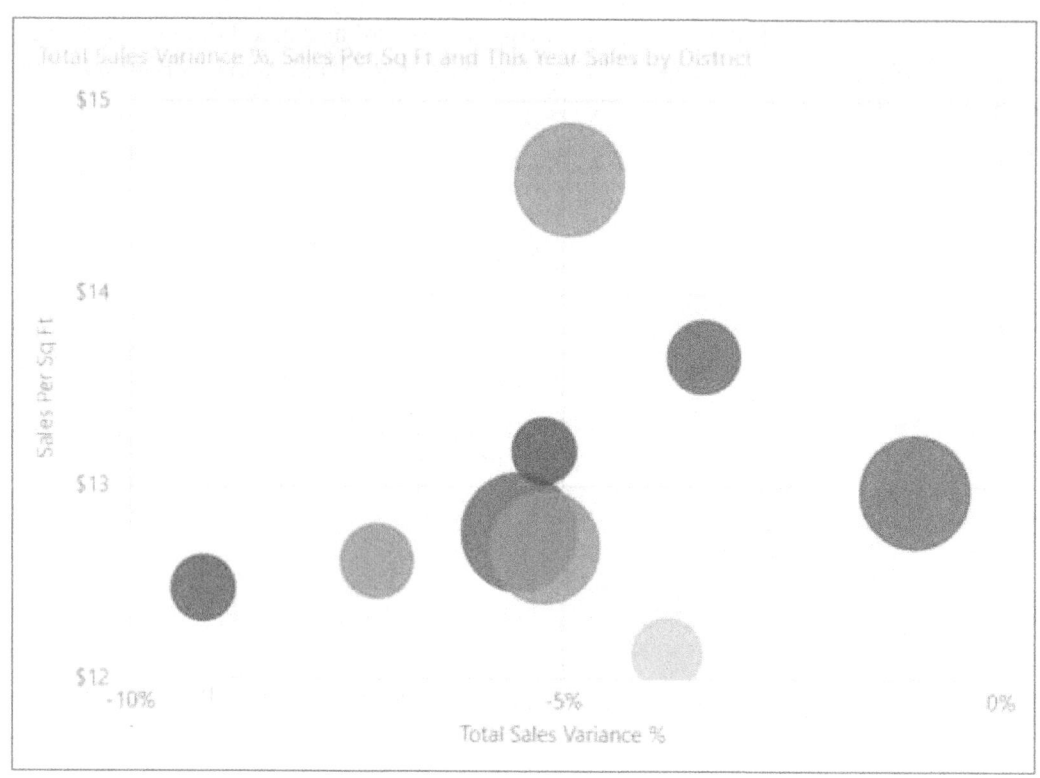

Both scatter and bubble charts can also have a play axis, which can show changes over time.

A dot plot chart is similar to a bubble chart and scatter chart except that it can plot numerical or categorical data along the X axis. This example happens to use squares instead of circles and plots sales along the X axis.

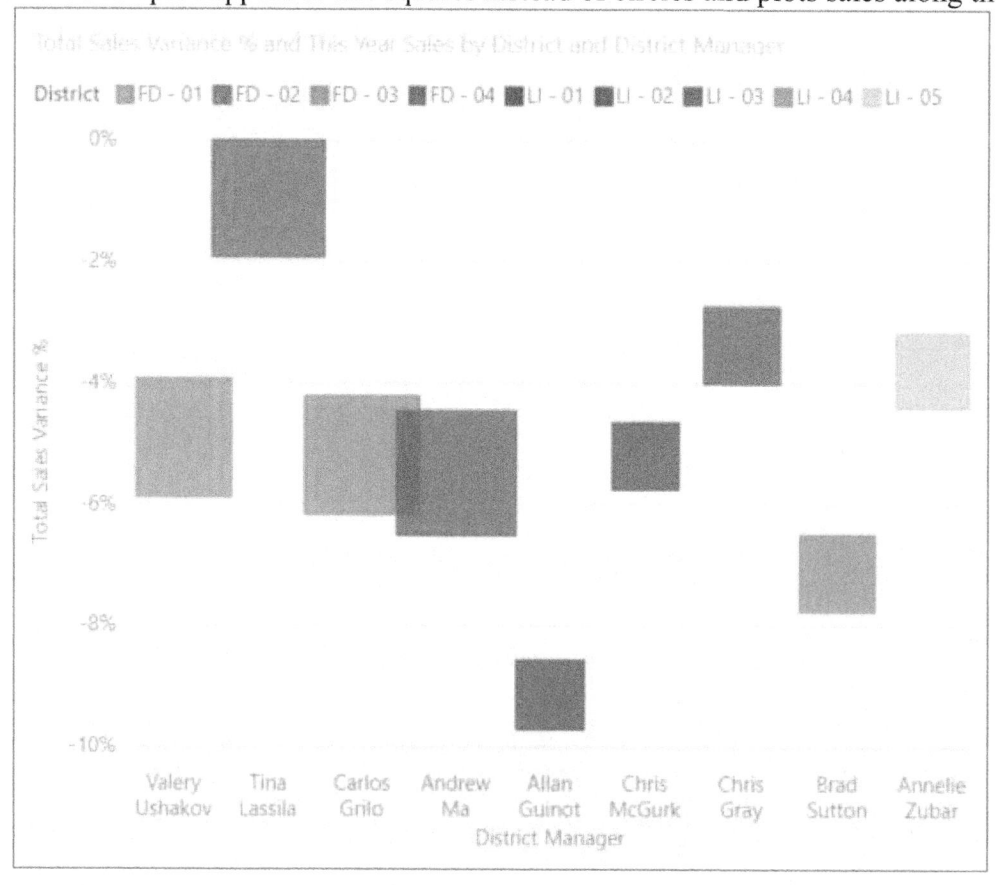

Scatter-high density

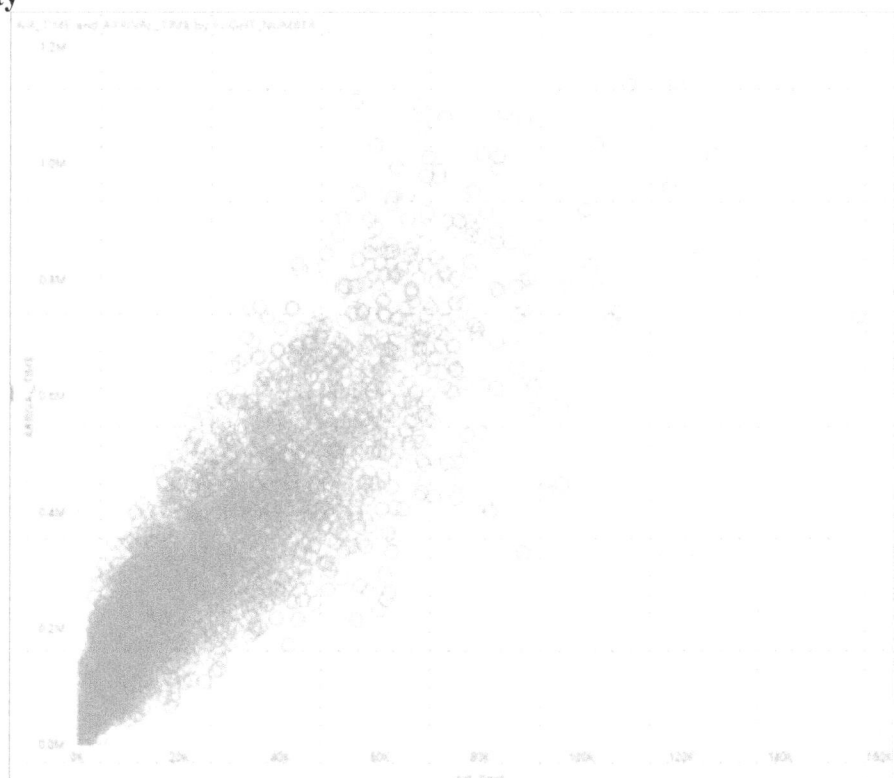

By definition, high-density data is sampled to quickly create visuals that are responsive to interactivity. High-density sampling uses an algorithm that eliminates overlapping points, and ensures that all points in the data set are represented in the visual. It doesn't just plot a representative sample of the data.

This ensures the best combination of responsiveness, representation, and clear preservation of important points in the overall data set.

Slicers:

A slicer is a standalone chart that can be used to filter the other visuals on the page. Slicers come in many different formats (category, range, date, etc.) and can be formatted to allow selection of only one, many, or all of the available values.

Slicers are a great choice to:
- Display commonly used or important filters on the report canvas for easier access.
- Make it easier to see the current filtered state without having to open a drop-down list.
- Filter by columns that are unneeded and hidden in the data tables.
- Create more focused reports by putting slicers next to important visuals.

Smart narrative:

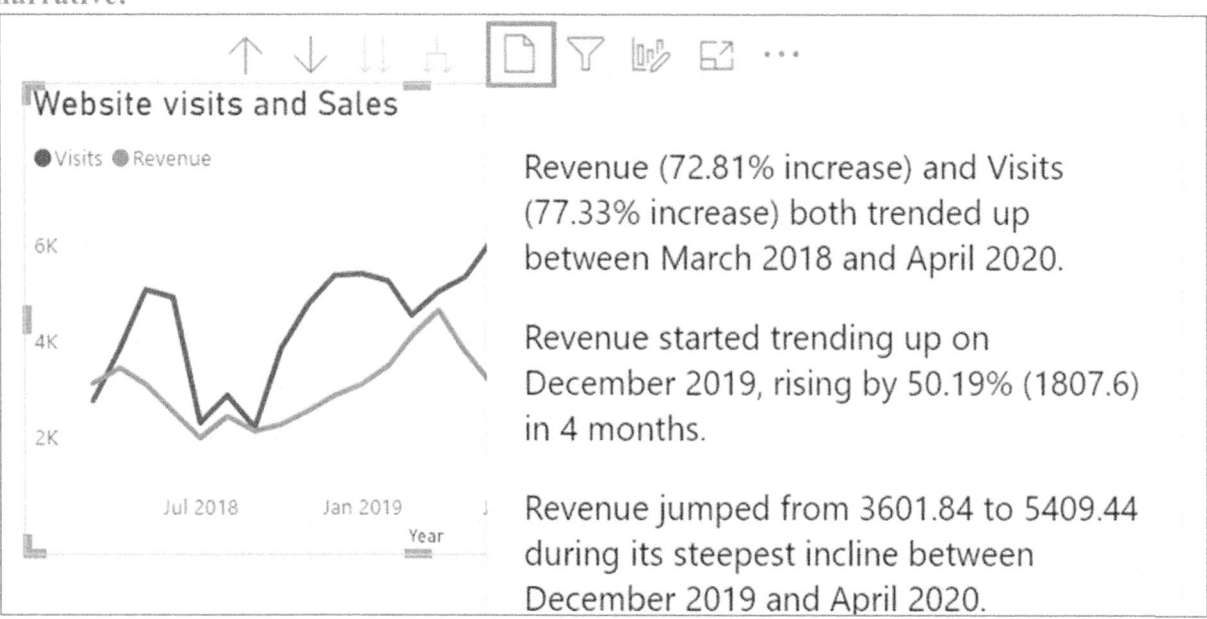

The smart narrative adds text to reports to point out trends, key takeaways, and add explanations and context. The text helps users to understand the data and identify the important findings quickly.

Standalone images:

A standalone image is a graphic that is added to a report or dashboard

Tables:

A table is a grid that contains related data in a logical series of rows and columns. It might also contain headers and a row for totals. Tables work well with quantitative comparisons where you are looking at many values for a single category. For example, this table displays five different measures for Category.

Tables are a great choice:
- To see and compare detailed data and exact values (instead of visual representations).
- To display data in a tabular format.
- To display numerical data by categories.

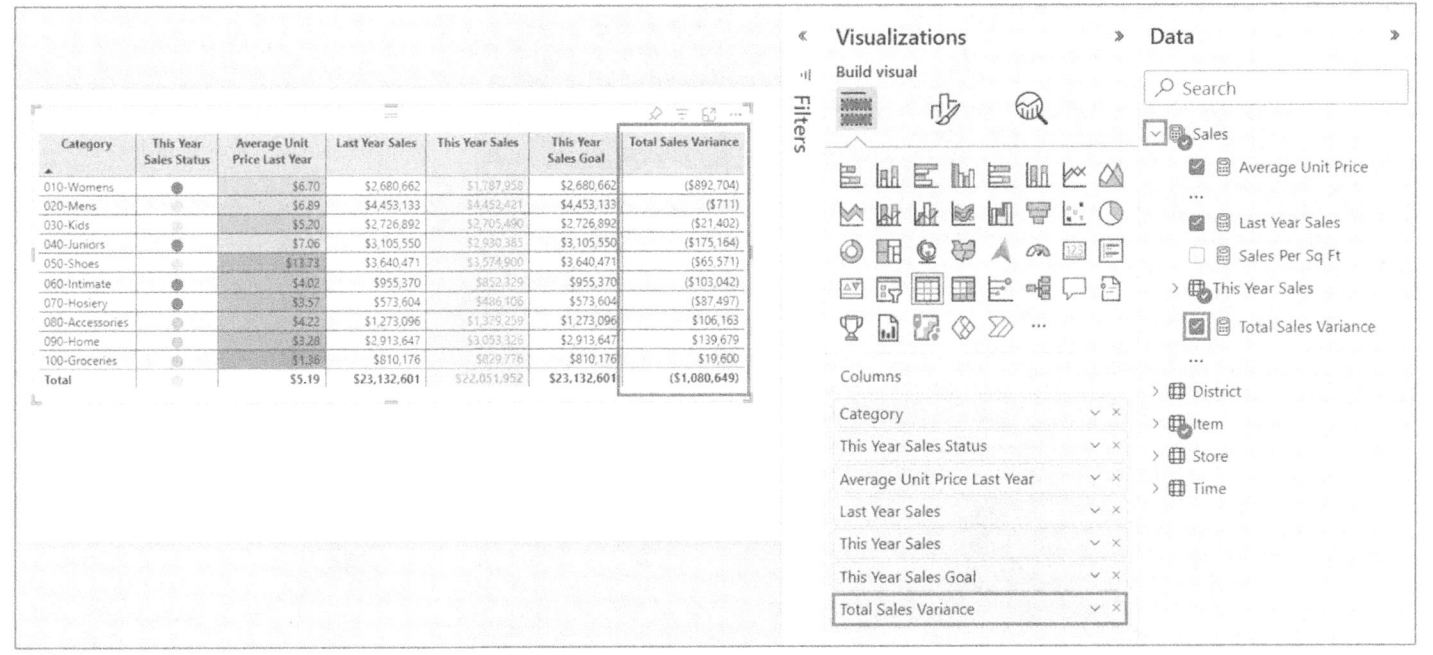

Category	This Year Sales Status	Average Unit Price Last Year	Last Year Sales	This Year Sales	This Year Sales Goal	Total Sales Variance
010-Womens	●	$6.70	$2,680,662	$1,787,958	$2,680,662	($892,704)
020-Mens	●	$6.89	$4,453,133	$4,452,421	$4,453,133	($711)
030-Kids	●	$5.20	$2,726,892	$2,705,490	$2,726,892	($21,402)
040-Juniors	●	$7.06	$3,105,550	$2,930,385	$3,105,550	($175,164)
050-Shoes	●	$13.73	$3,640,471	$3,574,900	$3,640,471	($65,571)
060-Intimate	●	$4.02	$955,370	$852,329	$955,370	($103,042)
070-Hosiery	●	$3.57	$573,604	$486,106	$573,604	($87,497)
080-Accessories	●	$4.22	$1,273,096	$1,379,259	$1,273,096	$106,163
090-Home	●	$3.28	$2,913,647	$3,053,326	$2,913,647	$139,679
100-Groceries	●	$1.36	$810,176	$829,776	$810,176	$19,600
Total	●	$5.19	$23,132,601	$22,051,952	$23,132,601	($1,080,649)

Treemaps:

Treemaps are charts of colored rectangles, with size representing value. They can be hierarchical, with rectangles nested within the main rectangles. The space inside each rectangle is allocated based on the value being measured. And the rectangles are arranged in size from top left (largest) to bottom right (smallest).

Treemaps are a great choice:
- To display large amounts of hierarchical data.
- When a bar chart can't effectively handle the large number of values.
- To show the proportions between each part and the whole.
- To show the pattern of the distribution of the measure across each level of categories in the hierarchy.
- To show attributes using size and color coding.
- To spot patterns, outliers, most-important contributors, and exceptions

Waterfall charts:

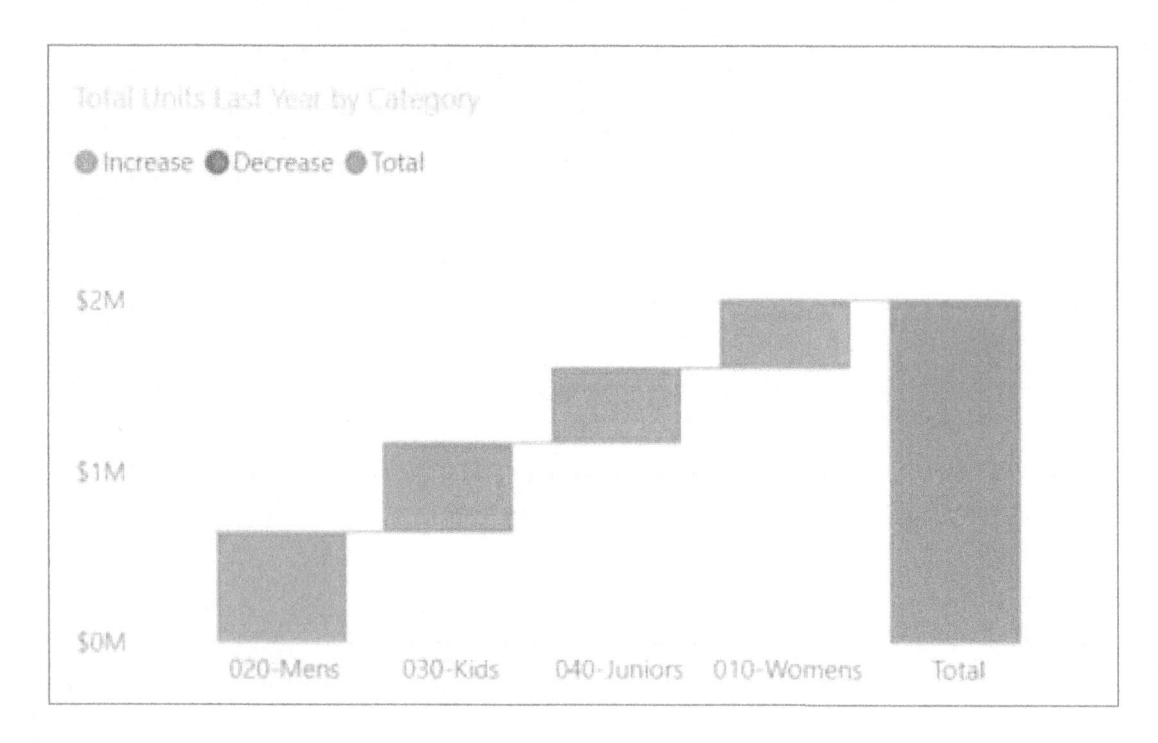

A waterfall chart shows a running total as values are added or subtracted. It's useful for understanding how an initial value (for example, net income) is affected by a series of positive and negative changes.

The columns are color coded so you can quickly tell increases and decreases. The initial and the final value columns often start on the horizontal axis, while the intermediate values are floating columns. Because of this "look", waterfall charts are also called bridge charts.

Waterfall charts are a great choice:
- When you have changes for the measure across time or across different categories.
- To audit the major changes contributing to the total value.
- To plot your company's annual profit by showing various sources of revenue and arrive at the total profit (or loss).
- To illustrate the beginning and the ending headcount for your company in a year.
- To visualize how much money you make and spend each month, and the running balance for your account.

2.9 Power BI Architecture

Power BI architecture is a service built on top of Azure. There are multiple data sources that Power BI can connect to. Power BI Desktop allows you to create reports and data visualizations on the dataset. Power BI gateway is connected to on-premise data sources to get continuous data for reporting and analytics. Power BI services refer to the cloud services that are used to publish Power BI reports and data visualizations. Using Power BI mobile apps, you can stay connected to their data from anywhere. Power BI apps are available for Windows, iOS, and Android platforms.

Power BI is a business platform that includes several technologies to work together. It delivers outstanding business intelligence solutions.

Power BI Architecture contains four steps.

Let us discuss these four steps giving insightful information about each one of them.
1. Data Integration
2. Data Transforming
3. Report & Publish
4. Creating and Dashboard

1. Data Integration:

Data is extracted from different sources which can be different servers or databases. The data from various sources can be in different types and formats. If you import the file into the Power BI, it compresses the data sets up to

1GB, and it uses a direct query if the compressed data sets exceed more than 1GB. Then the data is integrated into a standard format and stored at a place called a staging area. There are two choices for big data sets. They are as follows.
- Azure Analytics Services
- Power BI premium

2. Data Transforming:
Integrated data is not ready to visualize data because the data should be transformed. To transform the data, it should be cleaned or pre-processed. For example, redundant or missing values are removed from the data sets. After data is pre-processed or cleaned, business rules are applied to transform the data. After processing the data, it is loaded into the data warehouse.

3. Report & Publish:
After sourcing and cleaning the data, you can create the reports. Reports are the visualization of the data in the form of slicers, graphs, and charts. Power BI offers a lot of custom visualization to create the reports. After creating reports, you can publish them to power bi services and also publish them to an on-premise power bi server.

4. Creating Dashboards:
You can create dashboards after publishing reports to Power BI services, by holding the individual elements. The visual retains the filter when the report is holding the individual elements to save the report. Pinning the live report page allows the dashboard users to interact with the visual by selecting slicers and filters.

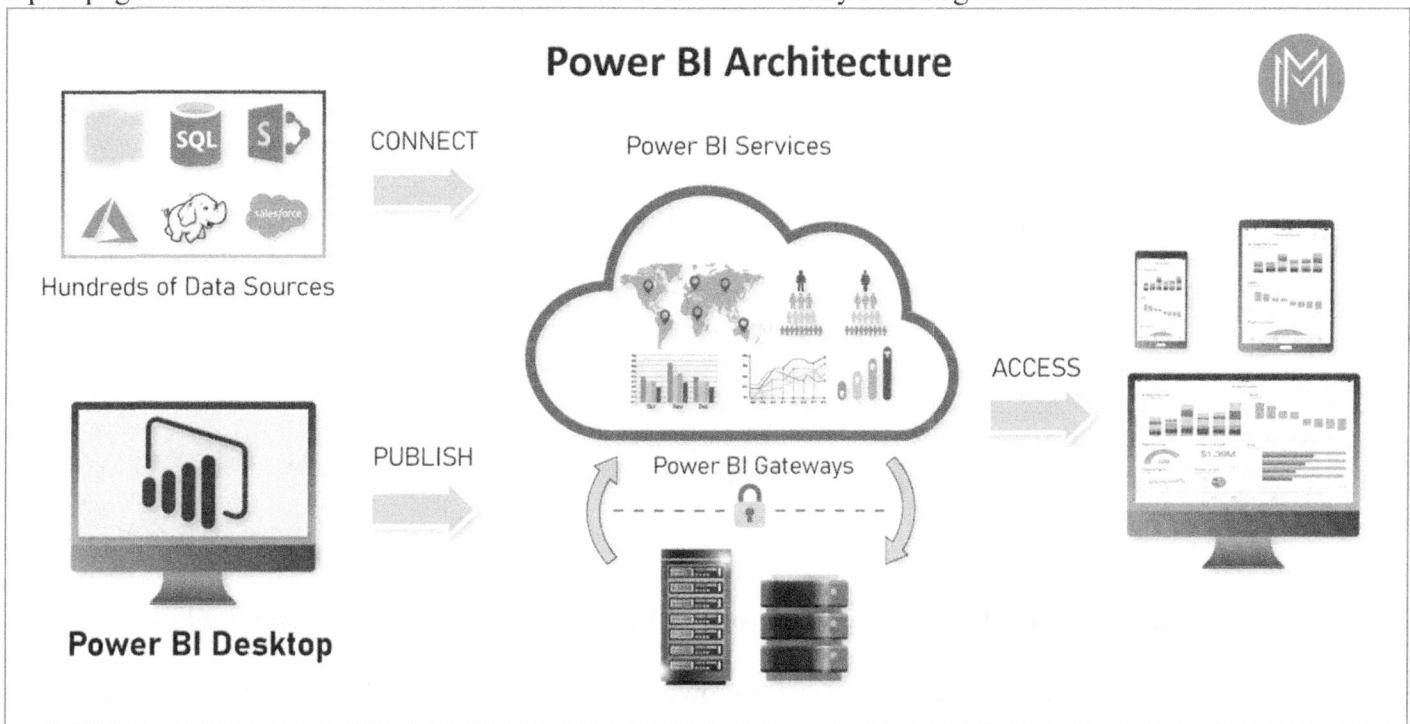

These are basic steps in the Power BI Architecture. Now we are going to discuss components of Power BI and how they work together in the Power BI Architecture.

Power BI Architecture - Working
We hope that you have understood the individual components of Power BI, and now, you will learn how these components work together. You will have a clear understanding of the Power BI Architecture with the help of the below image.

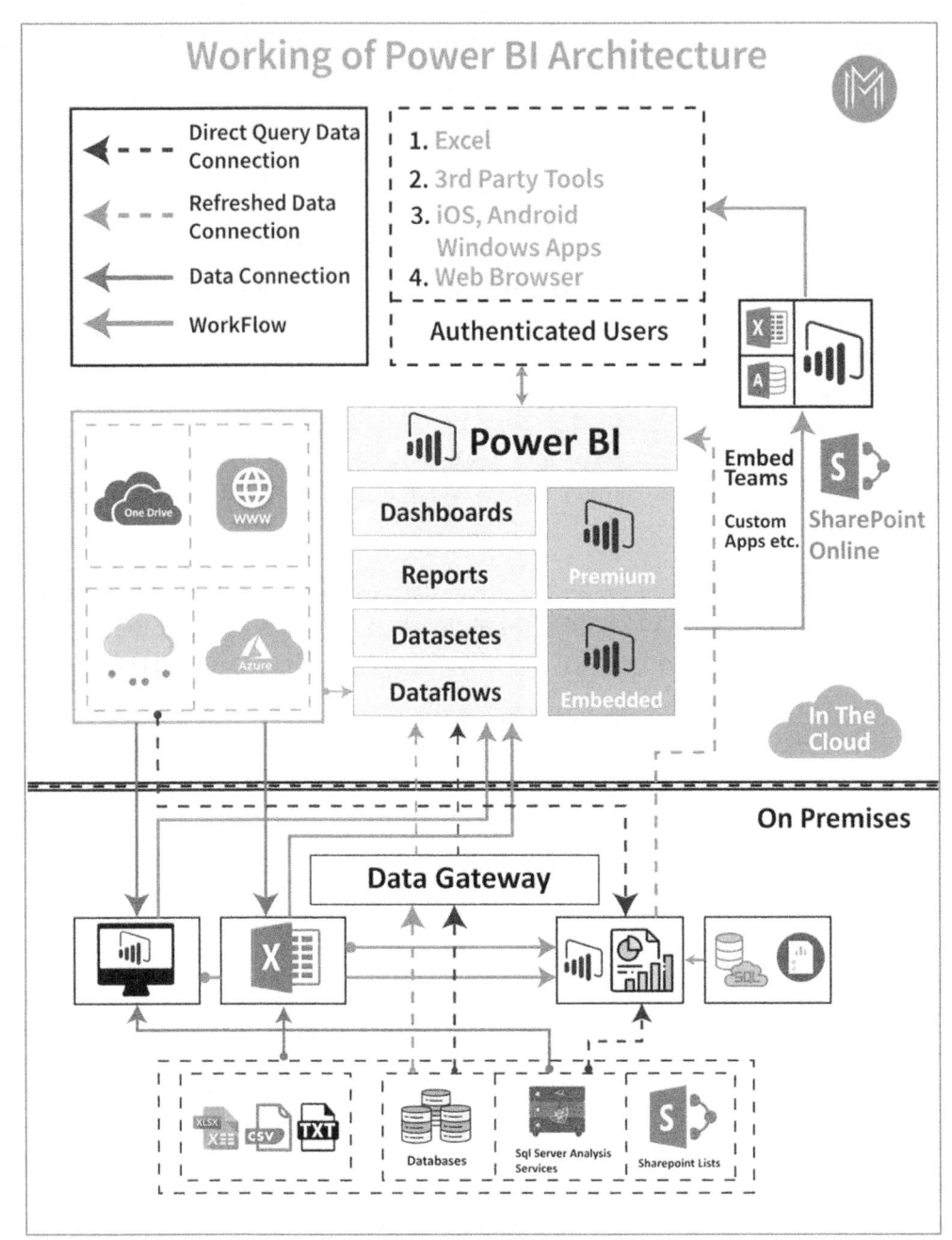

In the above diagram, it is clear that the upper half part represents On-Cloud services, and the lower half part represents the On-Premise services.

If you observe in the top of the image excel, web browsers and other sources are streaming into Power BI components, and they are called data sources. These data sources are authenticated users. Power BI has different data sources like On-Premise, Cloud databases, direct connections, etc.

On-Premise:
Power BI Desktop is accomplished with the authenticating, development and publishing tools. You can transfer the data from data sources to Power BI Desktop. And also, it allows users to create and publish reports on the Power BI Report Server or Power BI Service.

Power BI Publisher allows you to publish the Excel workbooks to the Power BI Report Server. Report Publisher and SQL server Data tools help in creating the KPIs, datasets, paginated reports, mobile reports, etc. All kinds of reports are published at the Power BI Report Server, and from there, reports are distributed to the end-users.

On-Cloud:

Power BI Gateway is the essential component in the Power BI architecture. The Power BI Gateway acts as a bridge or secure channel to transfer the data from On-premise data to On-cloud data sources or apps.
Cloud side architecture consists of a lot of components including Power suite having datasets, dashboards, reports, Power BI Premium, Power BI Embedded, etc. Users can embed the dashboards, reports into applications, SharePoint, Teams, etc. There are Cloud data sources and they are connected to the Power BI tools.

2.10 What is a Power BI Service?

Power BI service is a cloud-based business analytics and data visualization service that enables anyone to visualize and analyze data with greater speed, efficiency, and understanding. It connects users to a broad range of data through easy-to-use dashboards, interactive reports, and compelling visualizations that bring data to life.
The Power BI service website is built upon the azure cloud platform and adhere to HTML 5 standard. It has robust support for HTML5 via what is called PowerView.

The Data Sets for Power BI Service include
1. Uploaded Excel, CSV, or Power BI Desktop files.
2. Linked Excel, CSV, or Power BI Desktop files residing on OneDrive for Business or OneDrive Personal.
3. Data are available in your organization's content packs. Content packs are **"pre-packaged"** dashboards, datasets, and reports specific to your organization and are only available in Power BI Pro.
4. Data from other online services content packs; these services range from Bing to GitHub to MailChimp to SalesForce.
5. Data from SQL Azure Databases and Data Warehouses are also available, but it is also only available to Power BI Pro subscribers

What are the main features of Power BI Service?
The Main Features of Power BI Service UI are the following:
1. Navigation pane (left nav)
2. Canvas (in this case, dashboard with tiles)
3. Q&A question box
4. Icon buttons, including help and feedback
5. Dashboard title (navigation path, aka breadcrumbs)
6. Office 365 app launcher
7. Power BI home button
8. Labeled icon buttons

What are the Benefits of PowerBI Services?
Below are the key advantages of Power BI Services:
Integrates seamlessly with existing applications: Power BI integrates easily with your existing business environment allowing you to adopt analytics and reporting capabilities. Microsoft Azure consultants can also help you in leveraging this intuitive tool to embed interactive visuals in your applications easily.
Rich personalized dashboards: The crowning feature of Power BI is the information dashboards, which can be customized to meet the exact need of any enterprise. You can easily embed the dashboards and BI reports in the applications to provide a unified user experience.
Publish reports securely: The tool helps you to set up automatic data refresh and publish reports allowing all the users to avail of the latest information.
No memory and speed constraints: Shifting an existing BI system to a powerful cloud environment with Power BI embedded eliminates memory and speed constraints ensuring data is quickly retrievable and analyzed.

No specialized technical support required: Power BI provides agile inquiry and analysis without the need for specialized technical support. It supports a powerful natural language interface and the use of intuitive graphical designer tools.

Extracting business intelligence rapidly and accurately: It helps in transforming your enterprise data into rich visuals, thus extracting business intelligence for enhanced decision making.

Balanced simplicity and performance: The in-memory analysis technology and DAX scripting language are both exquisite examples of a balance between simplicity and performance.

Supports Advanced Data services: Microsoft Power BI tool can be integrated seamlessly with advanced cloud services like Cortana or Bot framework. Thus, providing results for the verbal data query given using natural language.

2.11 Power BI Service Architecture

In the previous section, you have learned how to publish the created reports in the Power BI Service. Power BI Service enables the users to create and access the reports, dashboards from the client platforms like mobile devices, websites, etc. User needs to interact with the Power BI Service whenever they want to access the data that is created on the Power BI. So, now, we will learn how the Power BI Service works.

Power BI Service Architecture consists of two clusters. The following are the two clusters.
- Front End Cluster
- Back End Cluster

Now, we will discuss the two clusters in detail.

1. Front End Cluster: Front end cluster acts as an intermediate between the back end cluster and the clients. It is also called a Web Front End Cluster. It establishes the initial connection and authenticates the users or clients using the Azure Active Directory. After user authentication, Azure Traffic Manager directs the user requests to the nearest data centers and Azure Content Delivery Network (CDN) allocates the statice files/content to the users or clients based on the geographical locations.

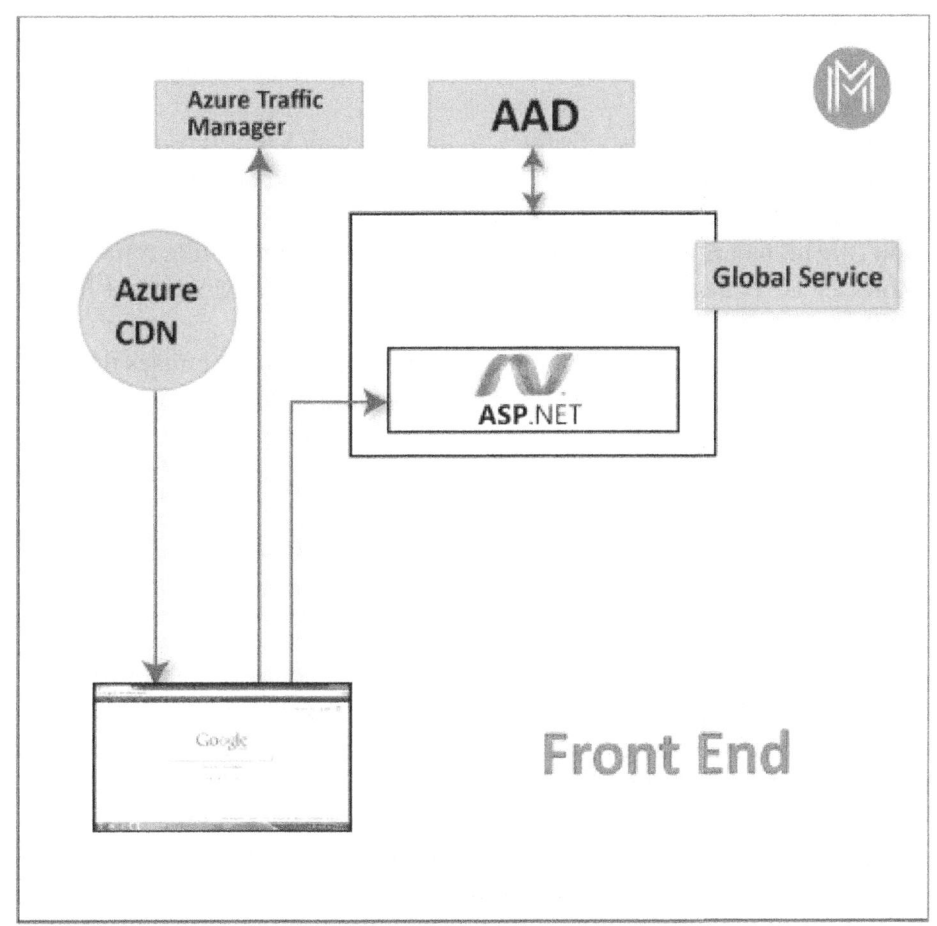

2. Back End Cluster: It manages the datasets, reports, storage, visualizations, data refreshing, data connections, and other services in the Power BI. At the back end cluster, the web client has only two direct points to interact with the data, i.e., Gateway Role and Azure API Management. These two components are responsible for authorizing, load balancing, routing, authentication, etc.

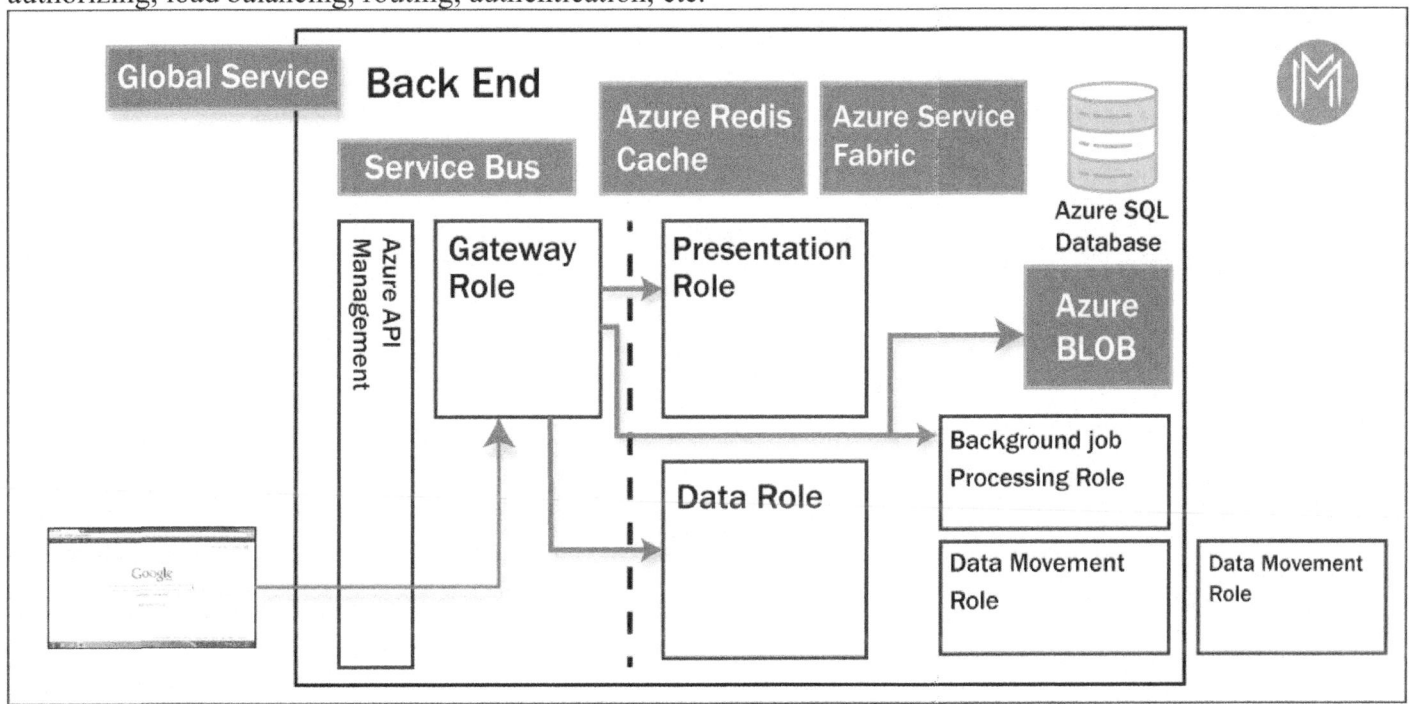

Working Of Power BI Service

- Power BI stores the data in two leading repositories, i.e., Azure SQL Database and Azure Block Storage. Azure Block Storage enables the users to store the datasets, and all system-related data and metadata are stored in the Azure SQL database.
- It authenticates the user requests and sends them to the Gateway Role. It processes the requests and assigns them to the appropriate components like Background Job Processing Role, Data Movement Role, Presentation Role, and Data Role.
- The presentation role manages all the associated visualization queries like reports and dashboards.
- Presentation Role sends requests to the Gateway Role to the Data Movement Role or Data Role for all relevant datasets.
- Azure Service Bus is used to connect and fetch the data from the On-Premises data sources with the cloud. It sends a request to execute the queries On-Premises data source and retrieve the data from its cloud service.
- The Azure Service Fabric allows all components and microservices which are related to the Power BI Service.
- Azure Cache helps in reporting the data that is stored in the in-memory of the Power BI system.

2.12 Power BI Dashboard

A Power BI dashboard is a single-page, interactive view that consolidates key metrics and visualizations from various reports and datasets into one cohesive layout. Dashboards are designed for quick insights and monitoring, enabling users to see a snapshot of business performance at a glance. Visualizations on a dashboard are generated from reports, and each report is based on one dataset. We all know that Power BI is one of the best BI tools, and many organizations are using this tool to generate reports and dashboards to make effective business decisions. Before using the Power BI services and features, you should know about the Architecture of Power BI, because you should know how the Power BI services, and components are being used to transform the data, and create the reports and dashboards.

Below are the examples of Dashboard published on Power BI Service

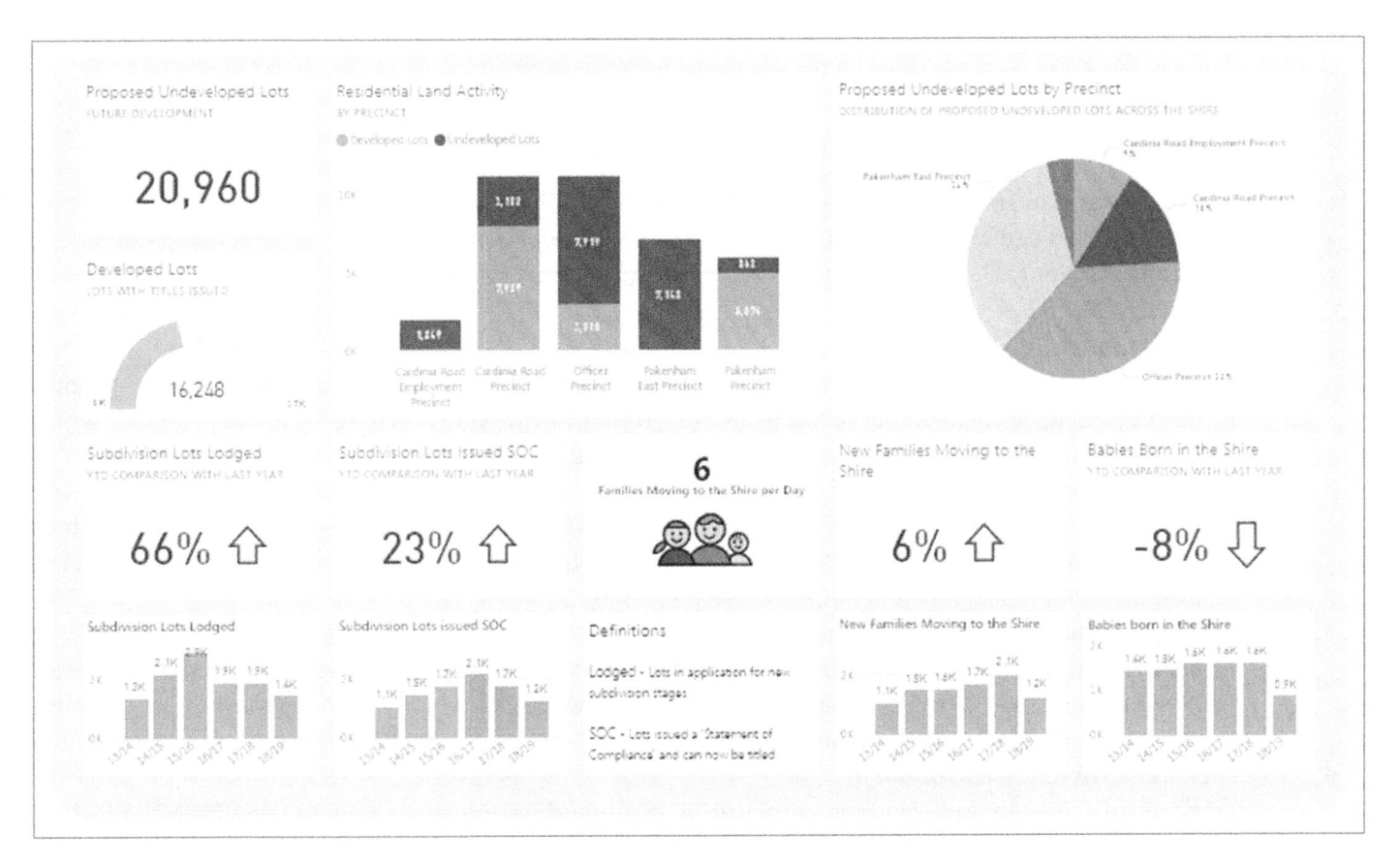

The visualizations you see on the dashboard are called Tiles and are pinned to the dashboard by report designers. Power BI allows you to create different reports on Power BI Desktop. These reports can be published on the Power BI dashboard using the Power BI service. A Power BI report created on Power BI Desktop can be published on to Power BI Service by clicking on the Publish button.

Key Features of a Power BI Dashboard
- **Single-Page View**: Displays multiple visualizations in one place.
- **Real-Time Data**: Can show live data updates for ongoing monitoring.
- **Interactivity**: Users can click on visualizations to explore underlying data.
- **Customizable Layout**: Users can arrange visuals to suit their needs.

Examples of Power BI Dashboards
1. **Sales Performance Dashboard**:
   - **Example**: A sales team creates a dashboard showing total sales, sales by region, product performance, and customer demographics. It helps the sales manager quickly assess which products are performing well and where to focus efforts.
2. **Financial Overview Dashboard**:
   - **Example**: The finance department uses a dashboard to display key financial metrics, such as revenue, expenses, profit margins, and cash flow. This allows executives to get a quick overview of the company's financial health.
3. **Marketing Campaign Dashboard**:
   - **Example**: A marketing team tracks various campaign metrics, including impressions, clicks, conversions, and ROI. The dashboard helps them visualize which campaigns are most effective and where to allocate future budget.
4. **Operational Efficiency Dashboard**:
   - **Example**: A manufacturing manager uses a dashboard to monitor production efficiency, machine downtime, and quality control metrics. This helps in identifying bottlenecks in the production process.
5. **Customer Satisfaction Dashboard**:
   - **Example**: A customer service team tracks customer feedback, net promoter score (NPS), and support ticket resolution times. The dashboard provides insights into customer satisfaction trends and areas for improvement.
6. **Project Management Dashboard**:
   - **Example**: A project manager uses a dashboard to visualize project timelines, budget usage, and task completion rates. This aids in tracking project progress and making informed decisions about resource allocation.

Benefits of Using Power BI Dashboards
- **Quick Insights**: Dashboards provide a fast overview of key performance indicators (KPIs).
- **Data-Driven Decisions**: Easy access to visual data aids in making informed decisions.
- **Increased Engagement**: Interactive elements keep users engaged and facilitate deeper exploration of the data.

Power BI dashboards serve as essential tools for monitoring business performance, providing a consolidated view of relevant data that helps organizations make timely and informed decisions.

Chapter 2: Installation of Power BI Desktop

2.1 Downloading Power BI Desktop

Power BI Desktop Downloading

The steps listed below and Screenshots will show you how to install the Power BI Desktop application.

Download the Power BI Desktop installation file from the
   https://www.microsoft.com/en-us/download/details.aspx?id=58494

Or

1. **Visit the Official Website:** https://www.microsoft.com/en-gb/power-platform/products/power-bi/
2. **Navigate to Power BI Desktop**: Click on the "Products" menu and select "Power BI Desktop" from the dropdown
3. **Click on Download**: On the Power BI Desktop page, look for the "Download Free" button and click it

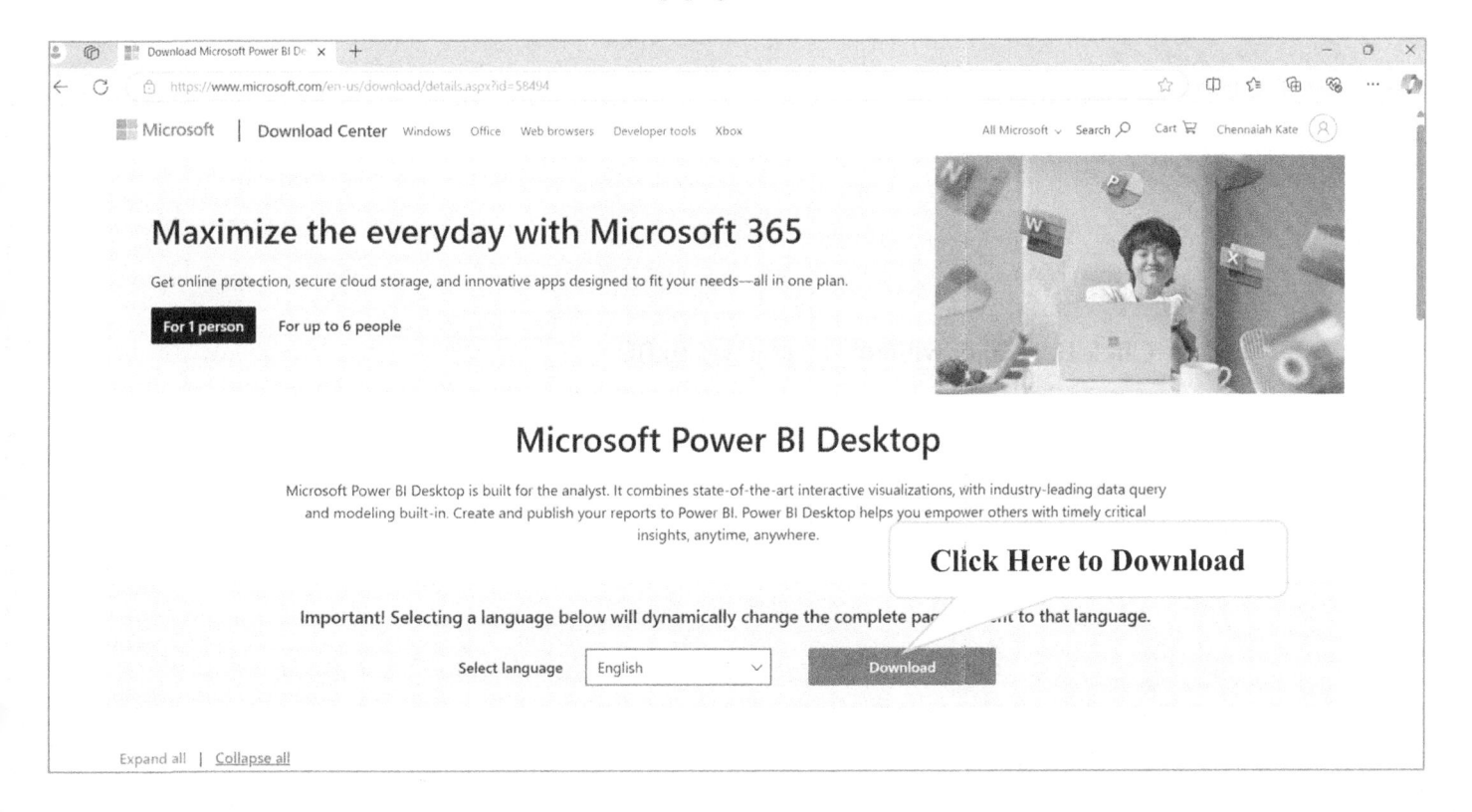

50

Choose the download you want

File Name	Size
☐ PBIDesktopSetup.exe	484.6 MB
☐ PBIDesktopSetup_x64.exe	527.3 MB

Select any one based your system configuration

Download Total size: 0 bytes

Choose the download you want

File Name	Size
☐ PBIDesktopSetup.exe	484.6 MB
☑ PBIDesktopSetup_x64.exe	527.3 MB

Click Here to download selected setup file

Download Total size: 527.3 MB

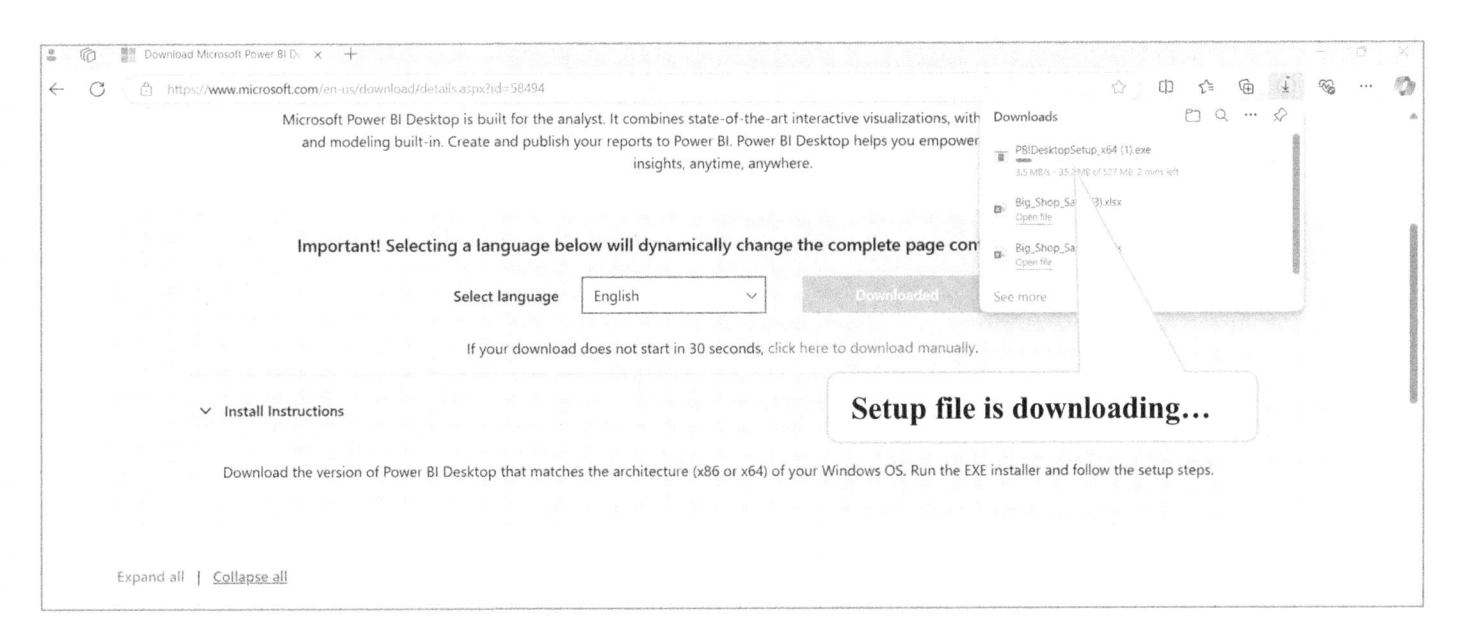

3.2 Power BI Desktop Installation

To install Power BI Desktop, follow these steps:
1. Launch the "installer" by double-clicking on it. Click next to continue.

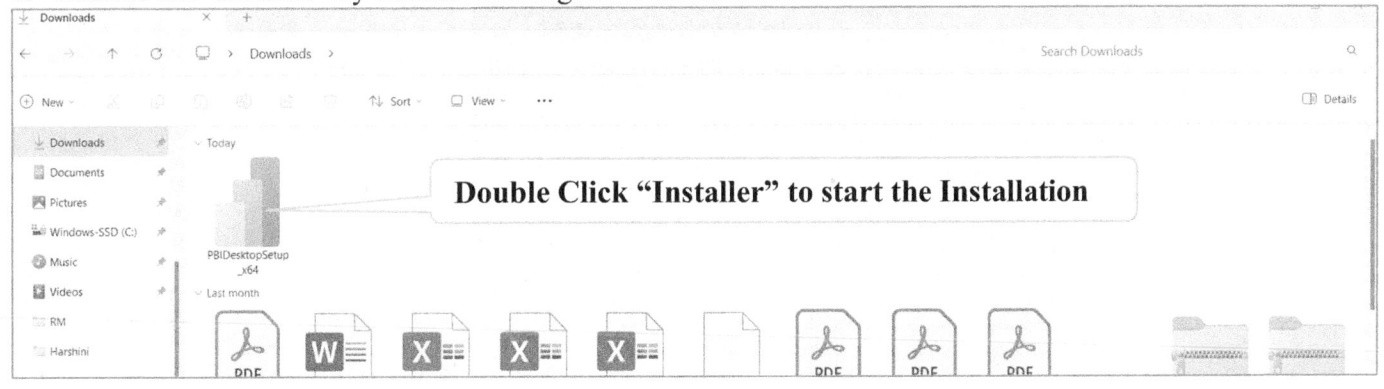

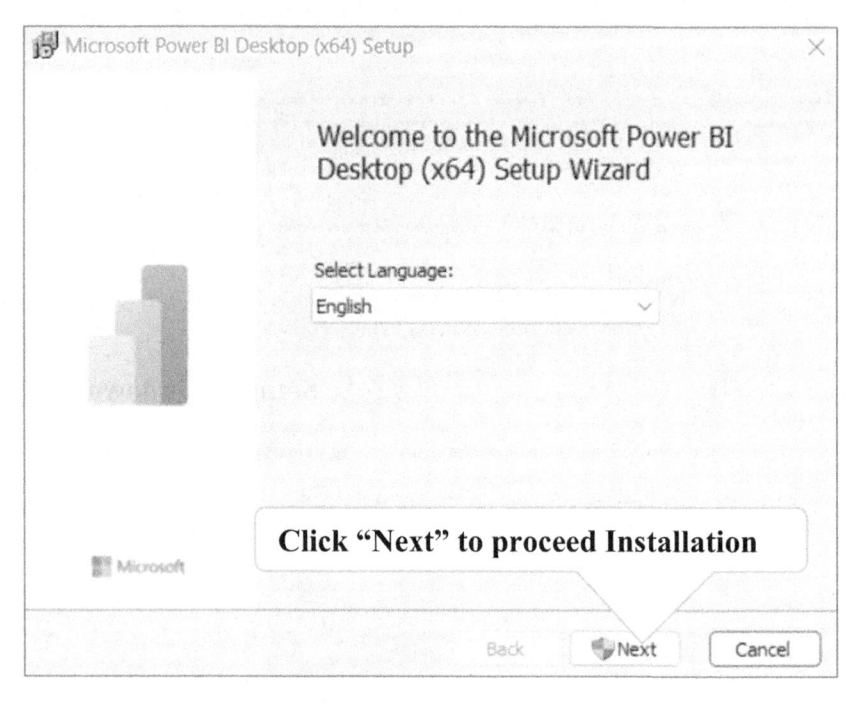

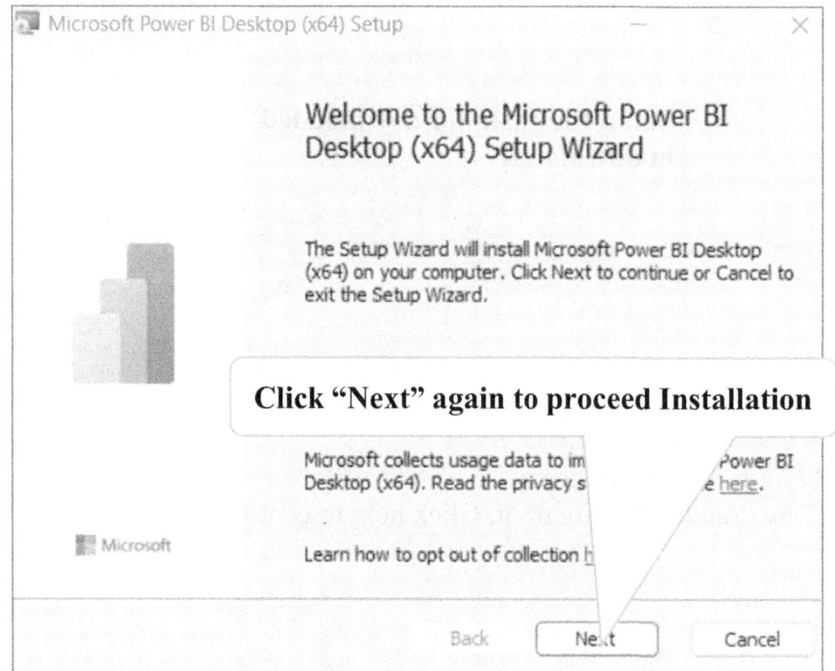

Screenshot: Microsoft Power BI Desktop (x64) Setup — Welcome screen with Select Language: English.

Click "Next" to proceed Installation

Screenshot: Microsoft Power BI Desktop (x64) Setup Wizard — second welcome screen.

Click "Next" again to proceed Installation

2. Read and accept the terms in the License Agreement. Click next to continue.

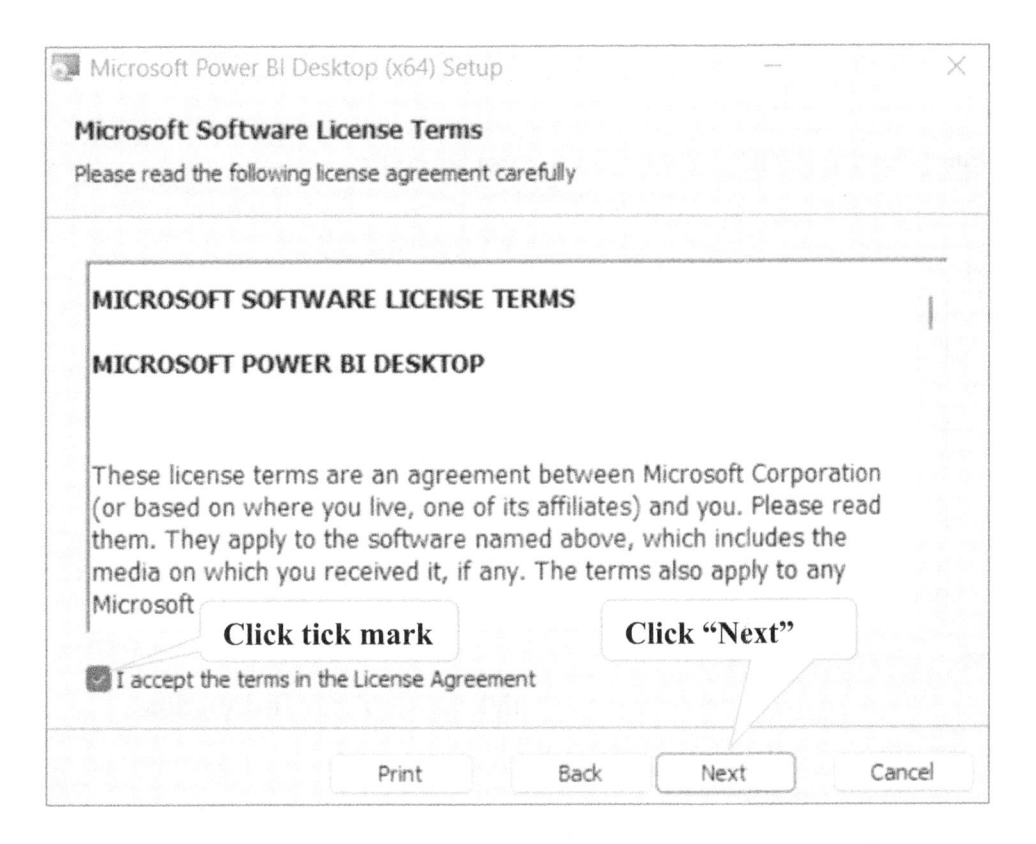

3. Select the installation folder location and click next to continue. Choose the default location or choose your location whenever you want. Click to next to continue and then click to install

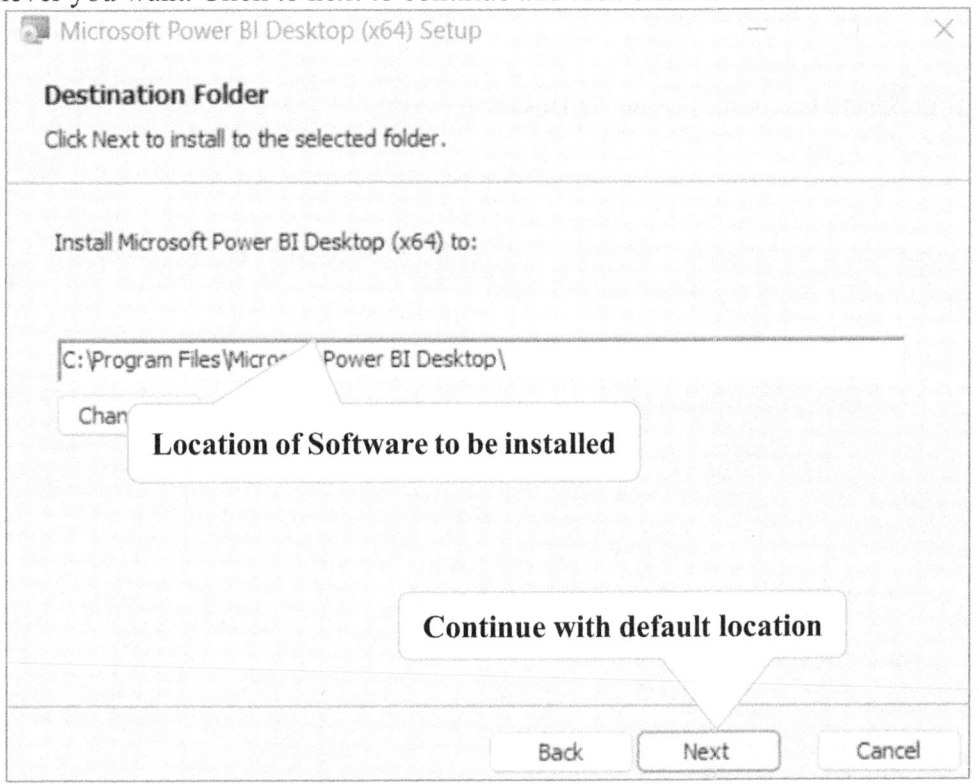

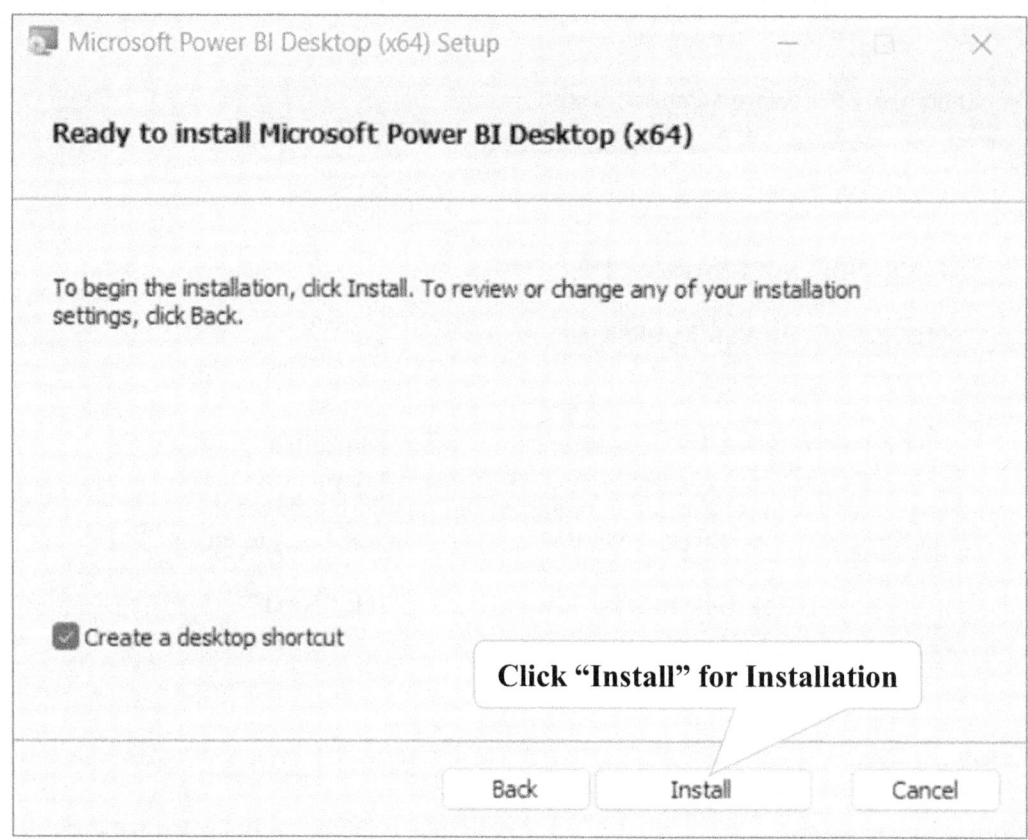

4. Power BI Desktop is installing, wait for some time

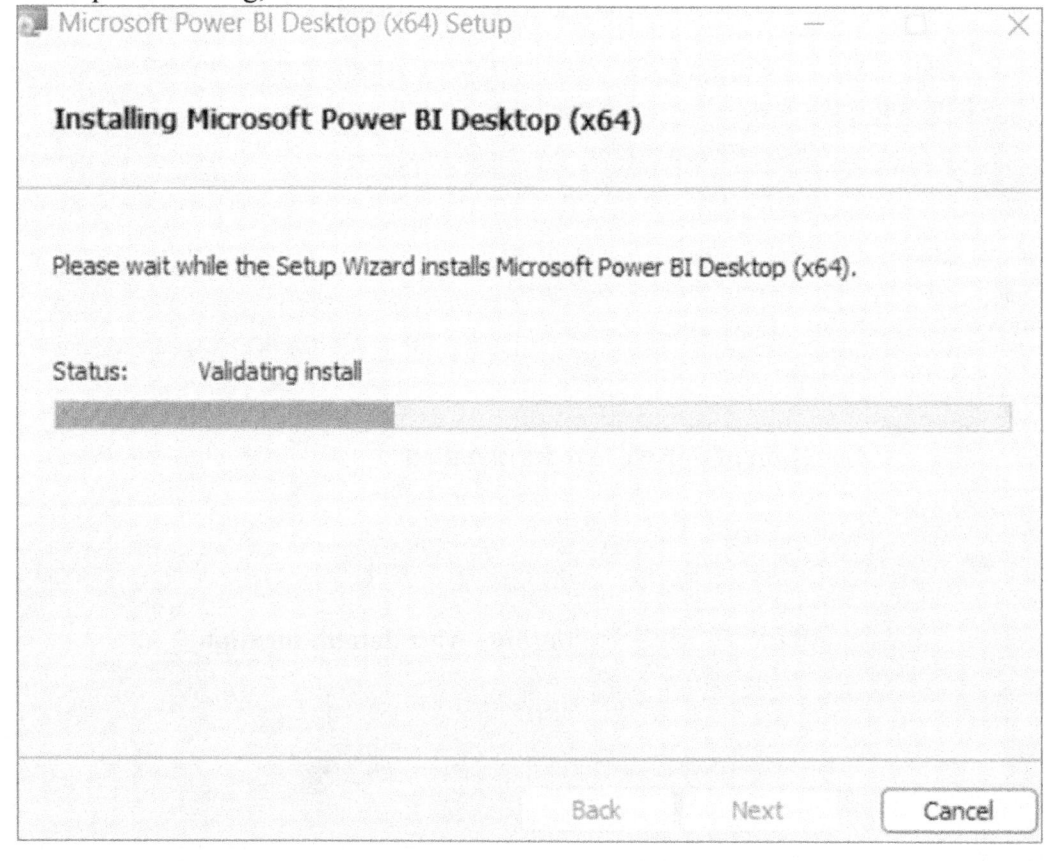

55

5. Click Finish to close the setup and launch the application

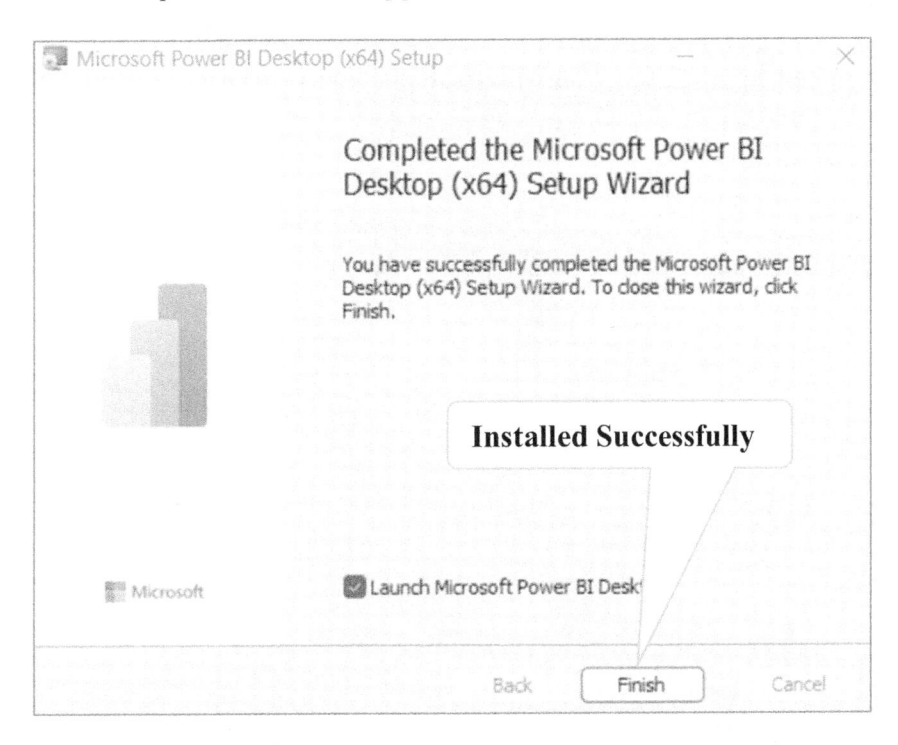

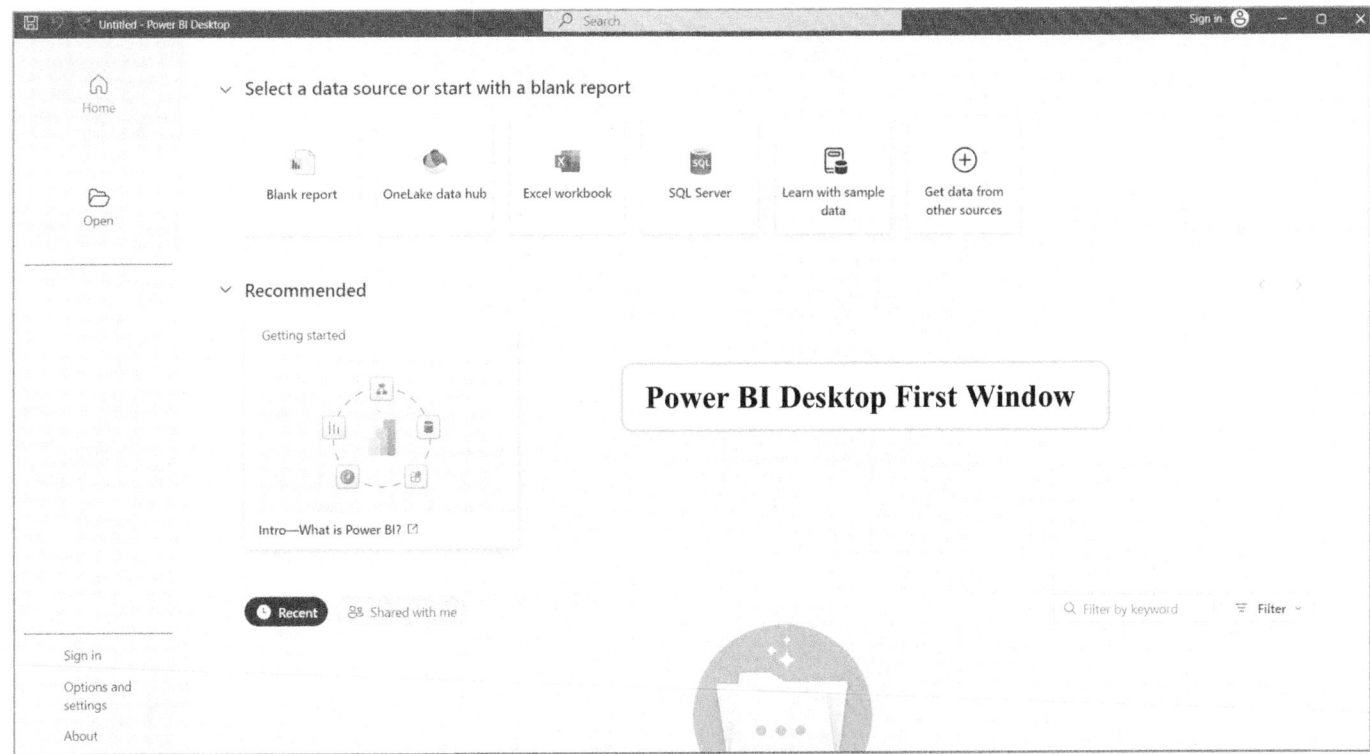

Installed Successfully

Power BI Desktop First Window

3.3 Launch Power BI Desktop

1. Once the installation is complete, find Power BI Desktop in your Start menu or applications folder and open it. Sign In (Optional) If prompted, sign in with your Microsoft account to access additional features.

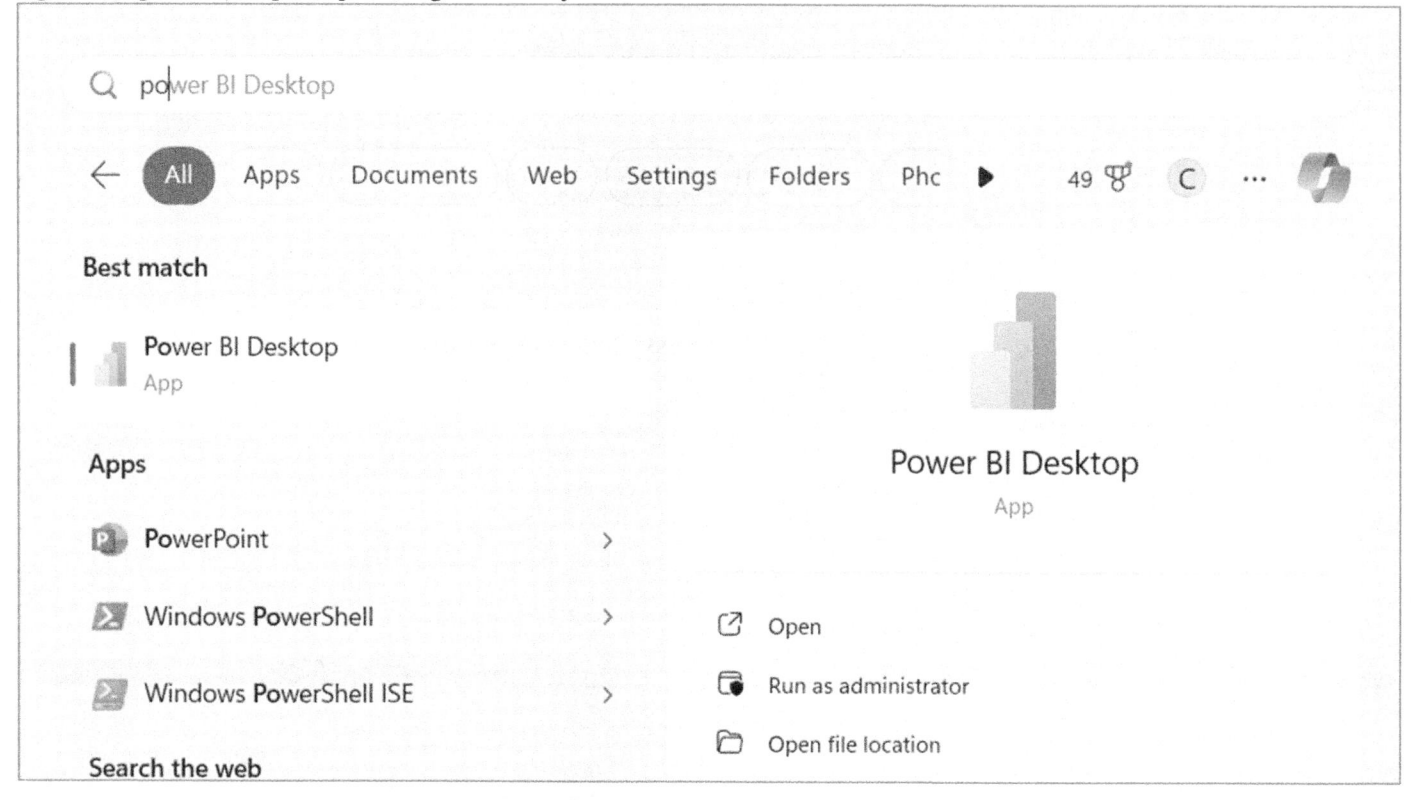

2. Select the data source, such as an Excel or SQL server.

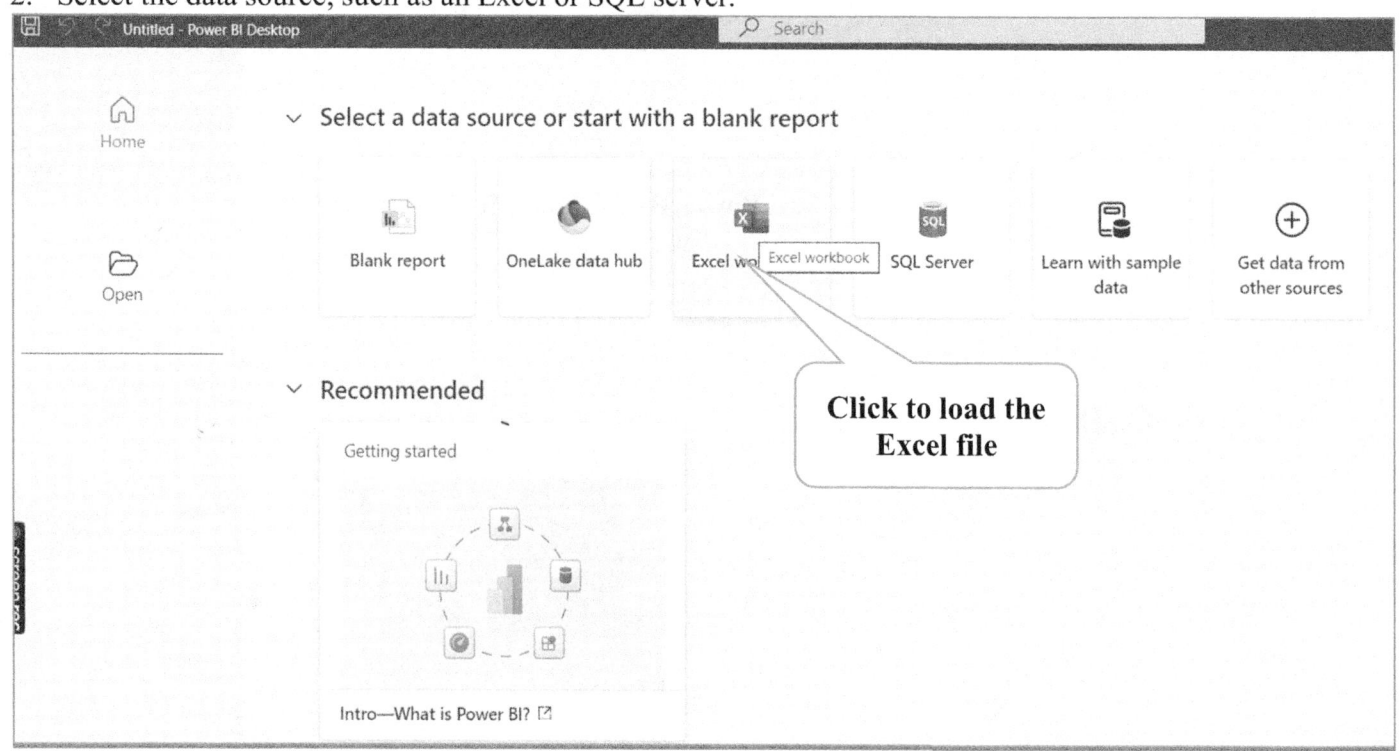

Click to load the Excel file

57

[Sample Excel File screenshot]

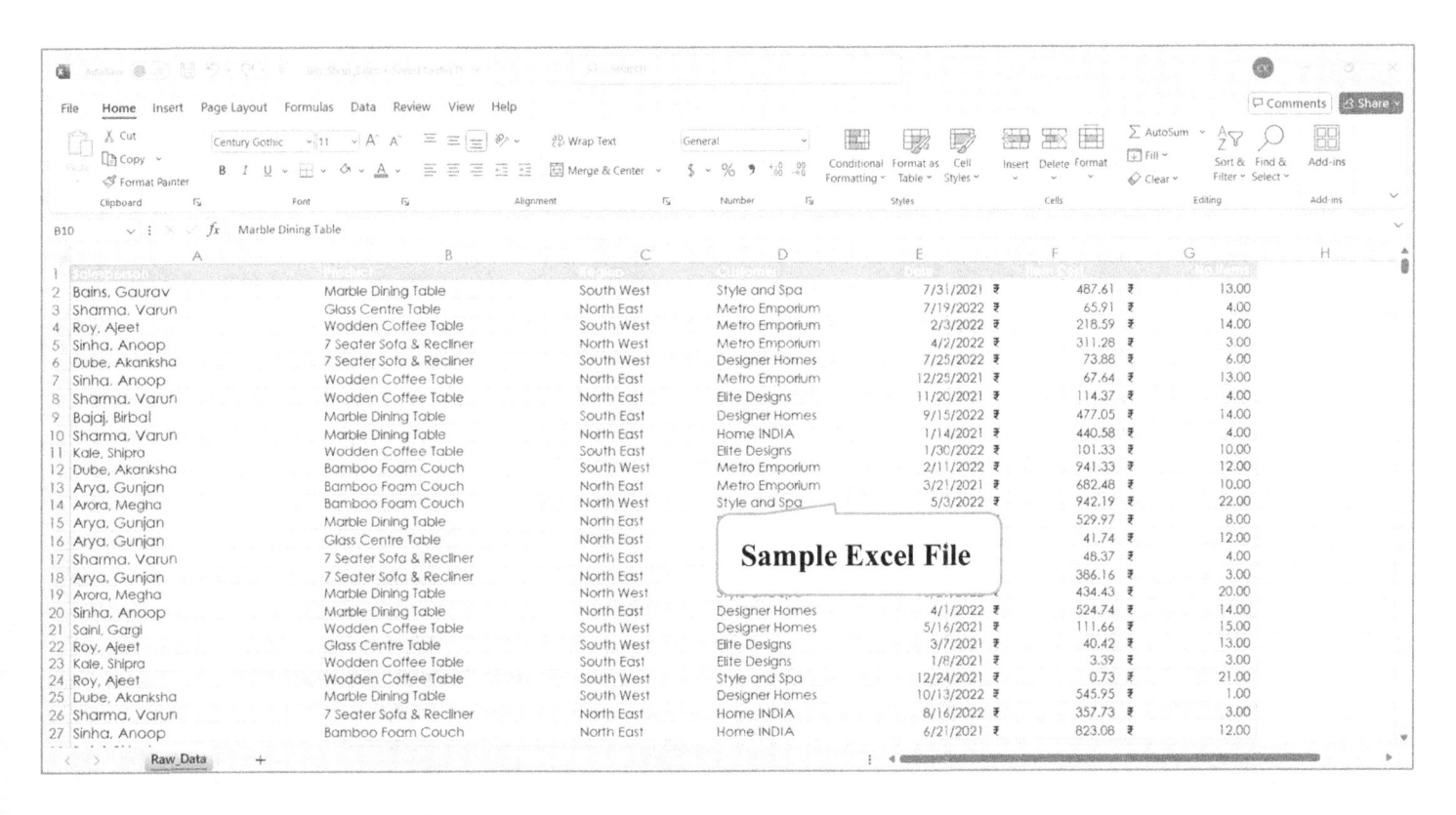

Sample Excel File

3. Choose the Excel file to load in Power BI application

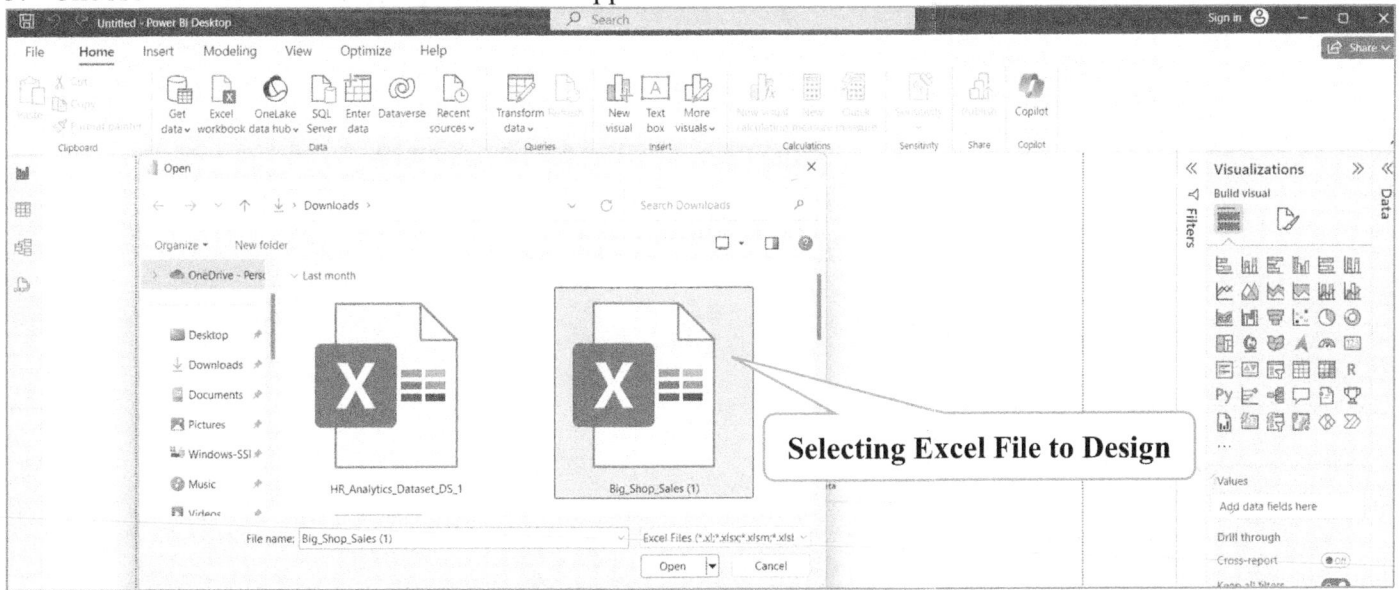

[Power BI Desktop screenshot with file open dialog]

Selecting Excel File to Design

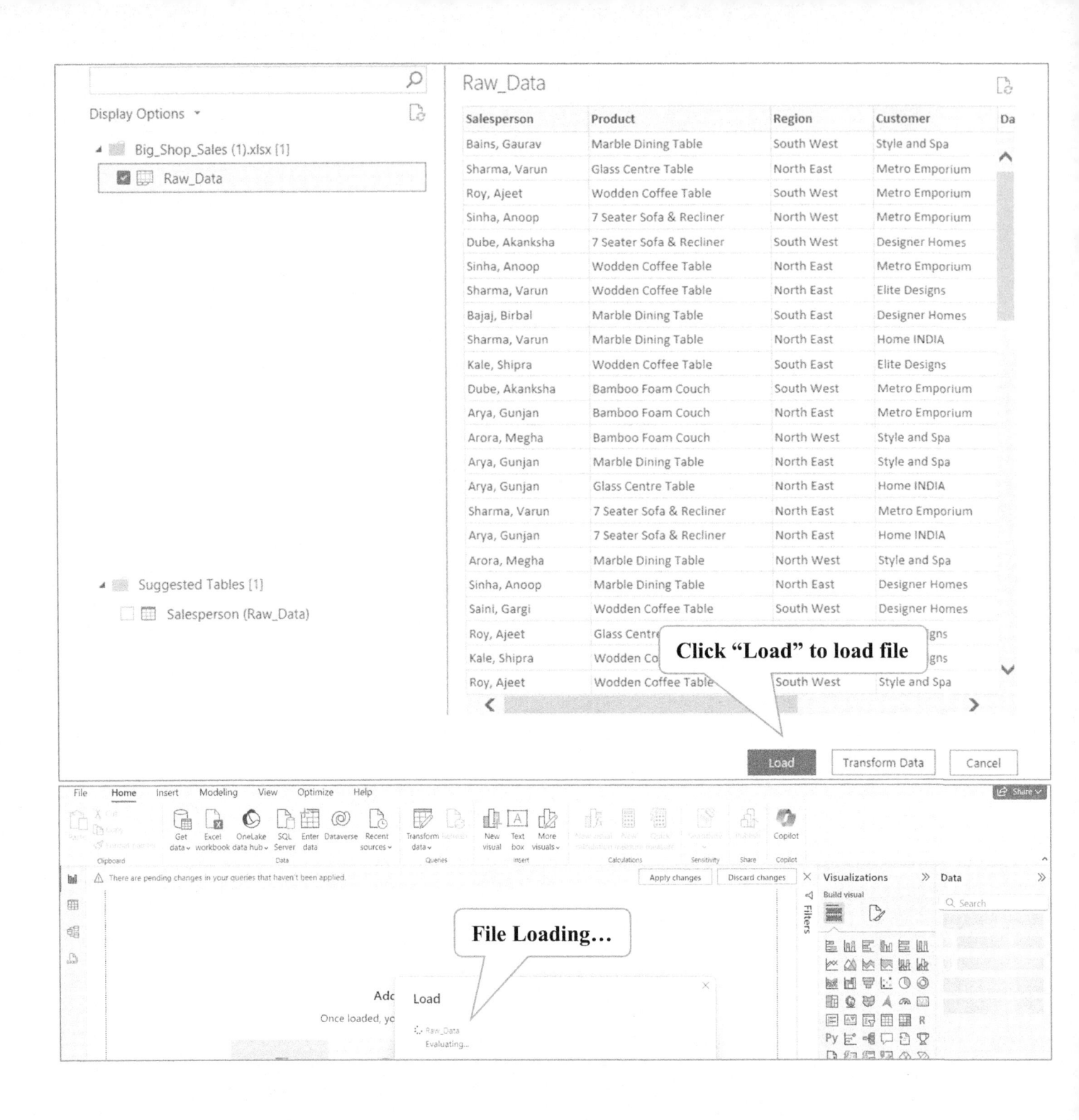

Salesperson	Product	Region	Customer
Bains, Gaurav	Marble Dining Table	South West	Style and Spa
Sharma, Varun	Glass Centre Table	North East	Metro Emporium
Roy, Ajeet	Wodden Coffee Table	South West	Metro Emporium
Sinha, Anoop	7 Seater Sofa & Recliner	North West	Metro Emporium
Dube, Akanksha	7 Seater Sofa & Recliner	South West	Designer Homes
Sinha, Anoop	Wodden Coffee Table	North East	Metro Emporium
Sharma, Varun	Wodden Coffee Table	North East	Elite Designs
Bajaj, Birbal	Marble Dining Table	South East	Designer Homes
Sharma, Varun	Marble Dining Table	North East	Home INDIA
Kale, Shipra	Wodden Coffee Table	South East	Elite Designs
Dube, Akanksha	Bamboo Foam Couch	South West	Metro Emporium
Arya, Gunjan	Bamboo Foam Couch	North East	Metro Emporium
Arora, Megha	Bamboo Foam Couch	North West	Style and Spa
Arya, Gunjan	Marble Dining Table	North East	Style and Spa
Arya, Gunjan	Glass Centre Table	North East	Home INDIA
Sharma, Varun	7 Seater Sofa & Recliner	North East	Metro Emporium
Arya, Gunjan	7 Seater Sofa & Recliner	North East	Home INDIA
Arora, Megha	Marble Dining Table	North West	Style and Spa
Sinha, Anoop	Marble Dining Table	North East	Designer Homes
Saini, Gargi	Wodden Coffee Table	South West	Designer Homes
Roy, Ajeet	Glass Centre Table		
Kale, Shipra	Wodden Coffee Table		
Roy, Ajeet	Wodden Coffee Table	South West	Style and Spa

Click "Load" to load file

File Loading...

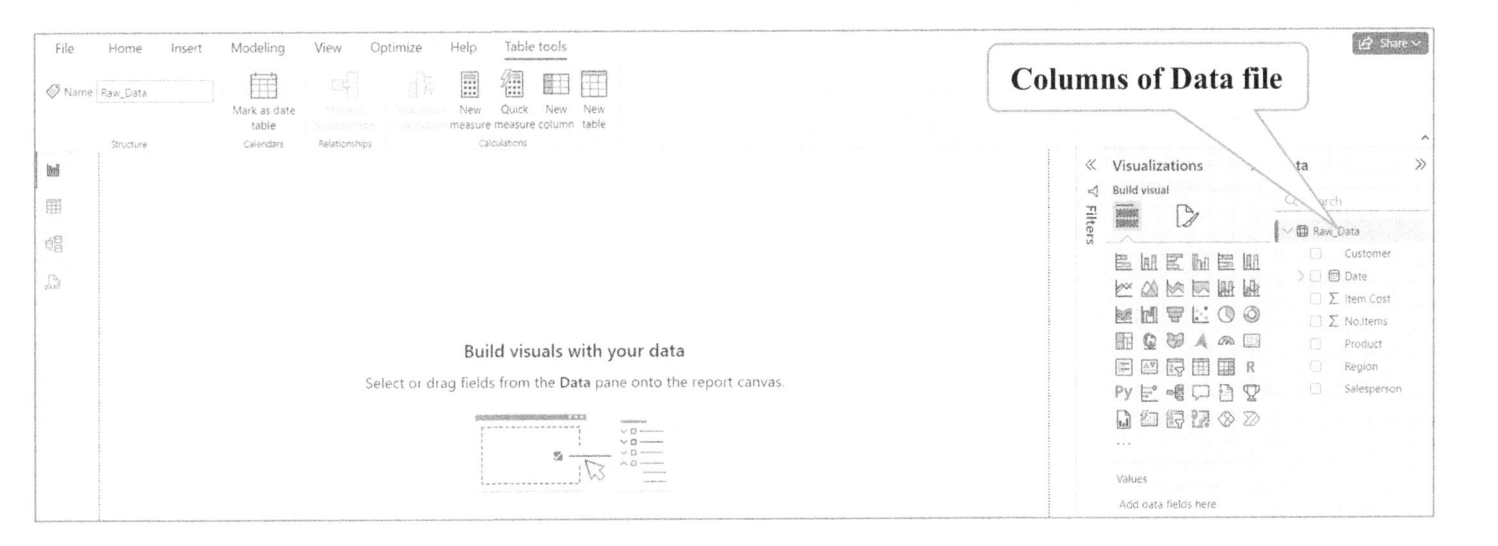

3.4 Power BI Desktop Window Icons and Buttons

We will see all the of the Desktop Window

First Horizontal Bar:
Save button, Undo, and Redo, Name of the designed file

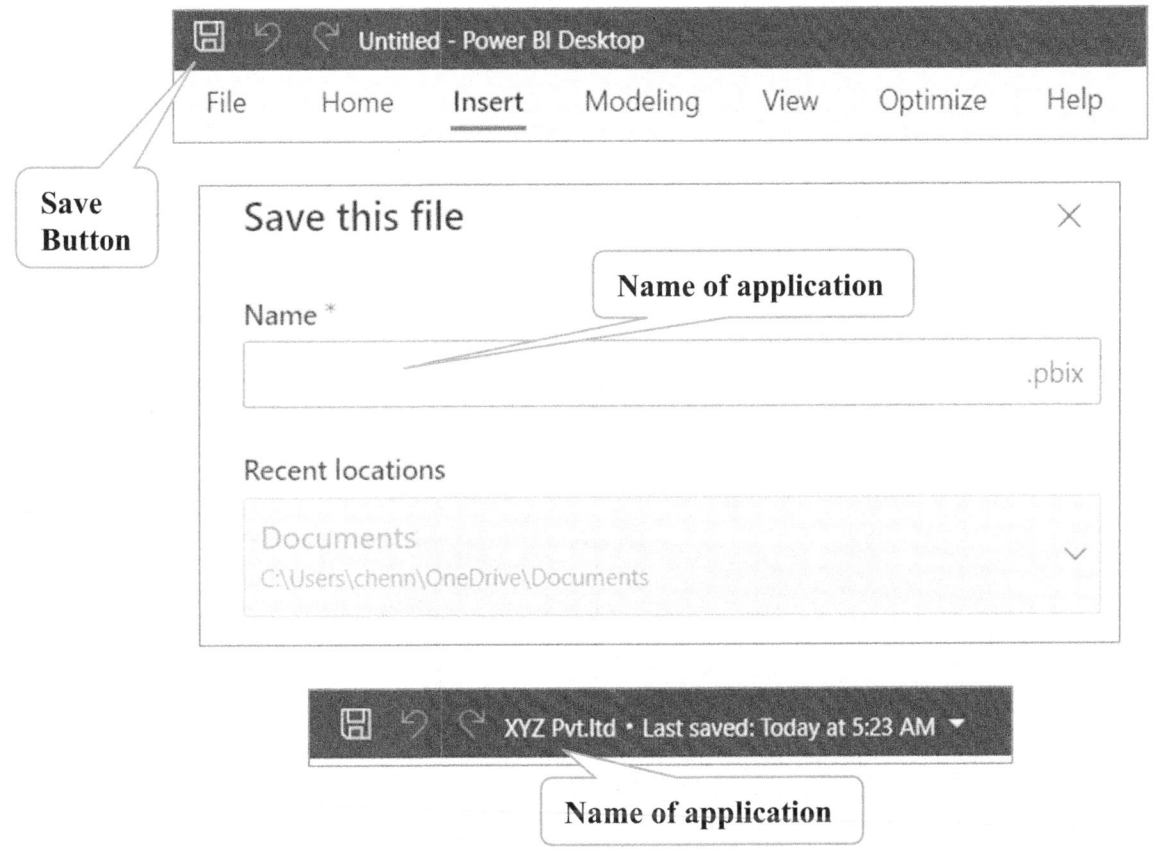

Bottom Horizontal Bar:
There are two types of modes, we can put on your design page. One is the Computer desktop View and Mobile view. You can design different reports on different pages like Page1, and Page 2, etc. like different sheets in Excel file

Ribbons Pane:

The ribbons pane is located at the window top horizontally and this pane has different ribbons such as File, Home, Insert, Modeling, View, Optimize and Help.

| File | Home | Insert | Modeling | View | Optimize | Help |

File ribbon pane:

The File pane in Power BI Desktop includes options for managing your Power BI files and configurations. Some main components:

1. **New**: Create a new Power BI report.
2. **Open**: Open an existing Power BI report (.pbix file) from your local machine or cloud storage.
3. **Save**: Save the current report.
4. **Save As**: Save the report under a different name or location.
5. **Import**: Import data or reports from other sources.
6. **Options and Settings**: Access settings for the application, including data load options, regional settings, and query options.
7. **Publish**: Publish your report to the Power BI service for sharing and collaboration.
8. **Export**: Export your report to various formats, such as PDF or PowerPoint.
9. **Close**: Close the current report.
10. **Recent Files**: A list of recently opened reports for quick access.

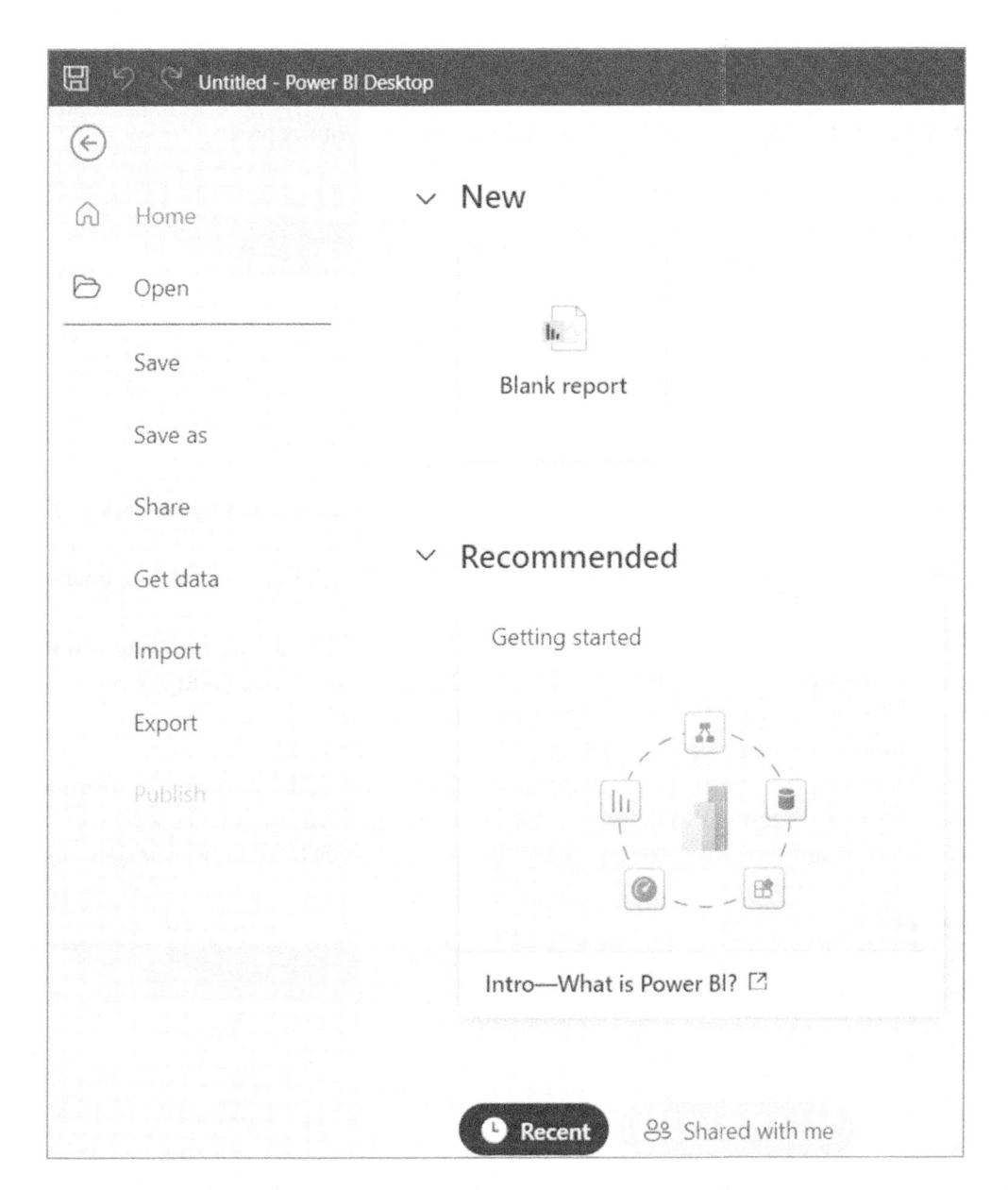

Home Pane:

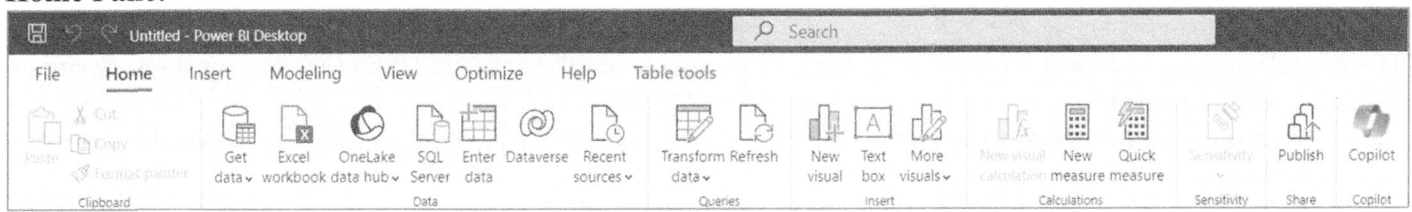

Home pane contains several key components that help users manage their reports and data. Some of the main components:
1. **Get Data**: This button allows you to connect to various data sources, such as Excel, SQL Server, and online services.
2. **Transform Data**: Opens Power Query Editor to clean and transform your data before loading it into your model.
3. **Recent Sources**: Displays a list of data sources you've accessed recently for quick access.
4. **Enter Data**: Allows you to manually enter data into a table.
5. **Refresh**: Refreshes the data in your report to reflect the latest changes.
6. **Publish**: This option lets you publish your report to the Power BI service for sharing and collaboration.
7. **New Report**: Starts a new report, allowing you to build visualizations from scratch.

8. **New Page**: Adds a new page to your report for organizing your visuals.
9. **View**: Options to change the view settings, such as switching between report view and data view.
10. **Clipboard**: Options for copying and pasting elements within your report.

Insert ribbon pane:

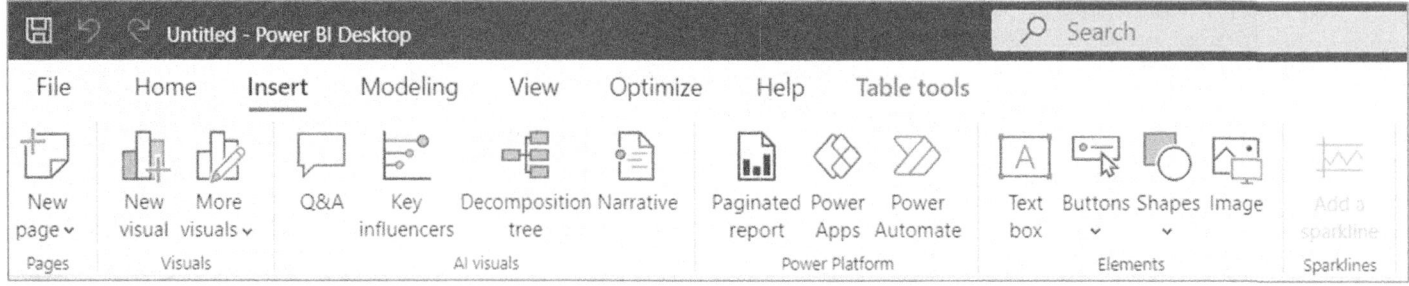

The Insert pane in Power BI Desktop provides various tools for adding elements to your report. Some of the main components are:
1. **Visualizations**: Allows you to insert various types of visualizations, such as bar charts, line charts, pie charts, tables, and more.
2. **Buttons**: Options to add buttons for navigation, bookmarks, or actions within your report.
3. **Shapes**: Insert shapes (rectangles, ellipses, etc.) to enhance report design and layout.
4. **Text Box**: Add text boxes for titles, descriptions, or annotations.
5. **Image**: Insert images to enrich your report with logos or other visuals.
6. **Video**: Embed videos from supported platforms to provide additional context or information.
7. **Web Content**: Add web content to display external web pages within your report.
8. **Smart Narrative**: Automatically generate insights and narratives based on your data visualizations.

Modeling ribbon pane:

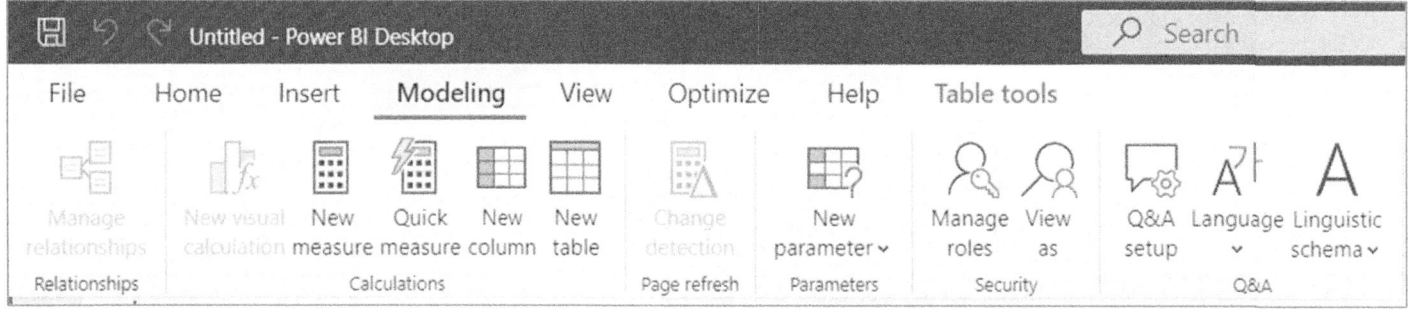

The Modeling pane in Power BI Desktop is focused on managing the data model and its relationships. Some of the main components are:
1. **Manage Relationships**: Allows you to view, create, edit, or delete relationships between tables in your data model.
2. **New Measure**: Create DAX measures to perform calculations on your data.
3. **New Column**: Add calculated columns to a table using DAX formulas.
4. **New Table**: Create a new table using DAX expressions or data from existing tables.
5. **Data Type**: Change the data type of selected columns (e.g., text, number, date).
6. **Format**: Format selected fields, including setting the display format for numbers and dates.
7. **Sorting**: Define sorting options for columns or tables.
8. **Hierarchy**: Create hierarchies to enable drill-down features in your visuals (e.g., Year > Quarter > Month).
9. **Column Tools**: Specific tools for managing columns, such as renaming or deleting.
10. **Table Tools**: Tools specific to managing tables, including the ability to set the primary key.

View Pane:

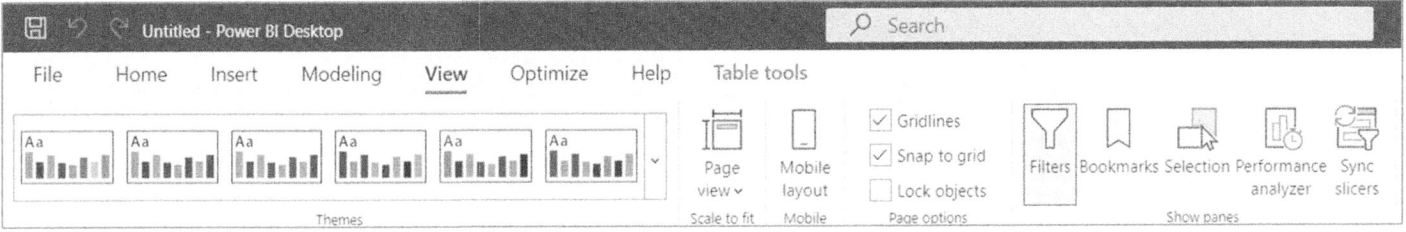

The View pane in Power BI Desktop allows you to control how you visualize your report and manage its layout. Here are the main components:
1. **Report View**: The primary mode for creating and editing your reports, where you design visuals on the canvas.
2. **Data View**: View and explore the data in your tables. This mode lets you inspect the underlying data.
3. **Model View**: Visualize and manage relationships between tables in your data model, allowing you to see how tables connect.
4. **Bookmarks Pane**: Manage bookmarks that save specific views of your report for easy navigation.
5. **Selection Pane**: View and manage the visibility of different elements and visuals on your report page.
6. **Sync Slicers**: Control the synchronization of slicers across multiple report pages for consistent filtering.
7. **Gridlines and Snap to Grid**: Toggle gridlines and enable or disable snapping visuals to the grid for precise alignment.
8. **Page View Options**: Adjust the size and orientation of the report canvas (e.g., Fit to Page, Actual Size).

Optimize pane:

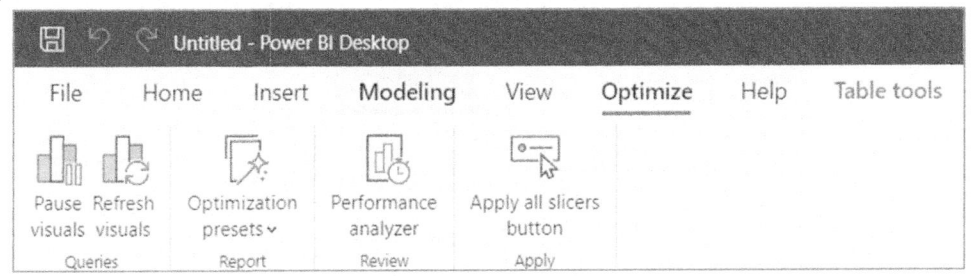

The Optimize pane in Power BI Desktop is focused on improving the performance of your reports and data models. Here are the main components you'll find in the Optimize pane:
1. **Performance Analyzer**: A tool that helps you track and analyze the performance of your report. It allows you to see how long visuals take to load and identify potential bottlenecks.
2. **Data Model Optimization**: Options and suggestions for optimizing your data model, such as reducing data size or simplifying relationships.
3. **Storage Mode**: Settings to control how data is stored and accessed, including options for DirectQuery and Import modes.
4. **Auto-Detect Relationships**: A feature that automatically identifies and suggests relationships between tables in your model.
5. **Aggregations**: Manage aggregations to improve query performance by pre-calculating summary data.
6. **Column Distribution**: View the distribution of data within columns to identify potential optimization opportunities.
7. **Query Diagnostics**: Analyze and troubleshoot issues with your data queries to enhance performance.

Table tools pane:

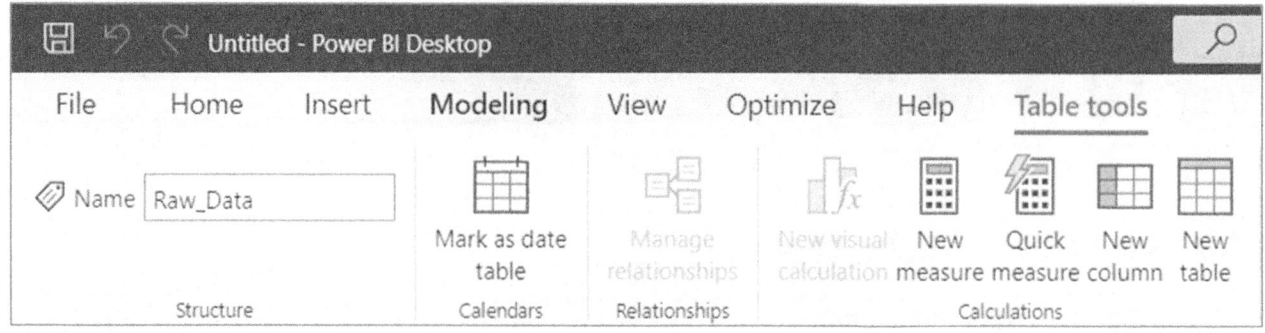

![Power BI Desktop ribbon showing Table tools tab with Name Raw_Data, Mark as date table, Manage relationships, New visual calculation, New measure, Quick measure, New column, New table]

The Table Tools pane in Power BI Desktop is specifically focused on managing tables in your data model. Here are the main components you'll find in the Table Tools pane:
1. **Table Name**: Allows you to rename the selected table for better organization.
2. **Data Type**: Change the data type of selected columns (e.g., text, number, date).
3. **Format**: Set the display format for selected columns, such as currency, percentage, or date formats.
4. **New Column**: Create a calculated column using DAX formulas.
5. **New Measure**: Add a new measure to perform calculations based on the data in the table.
6. **New Table**: Create a new table using DAX expressions or based on existing data.
7. **Sort By Column**: Set a specific column to determine the sorting order of another column.
8. **Remove Duplicate Values**: Identify and remove duplicate entries in the selected column.
9. **Data Preview**: View a preview of the data in the selected table.
10. **Relationships**: Manage relationships involving the selected table.

Visualization Pane:

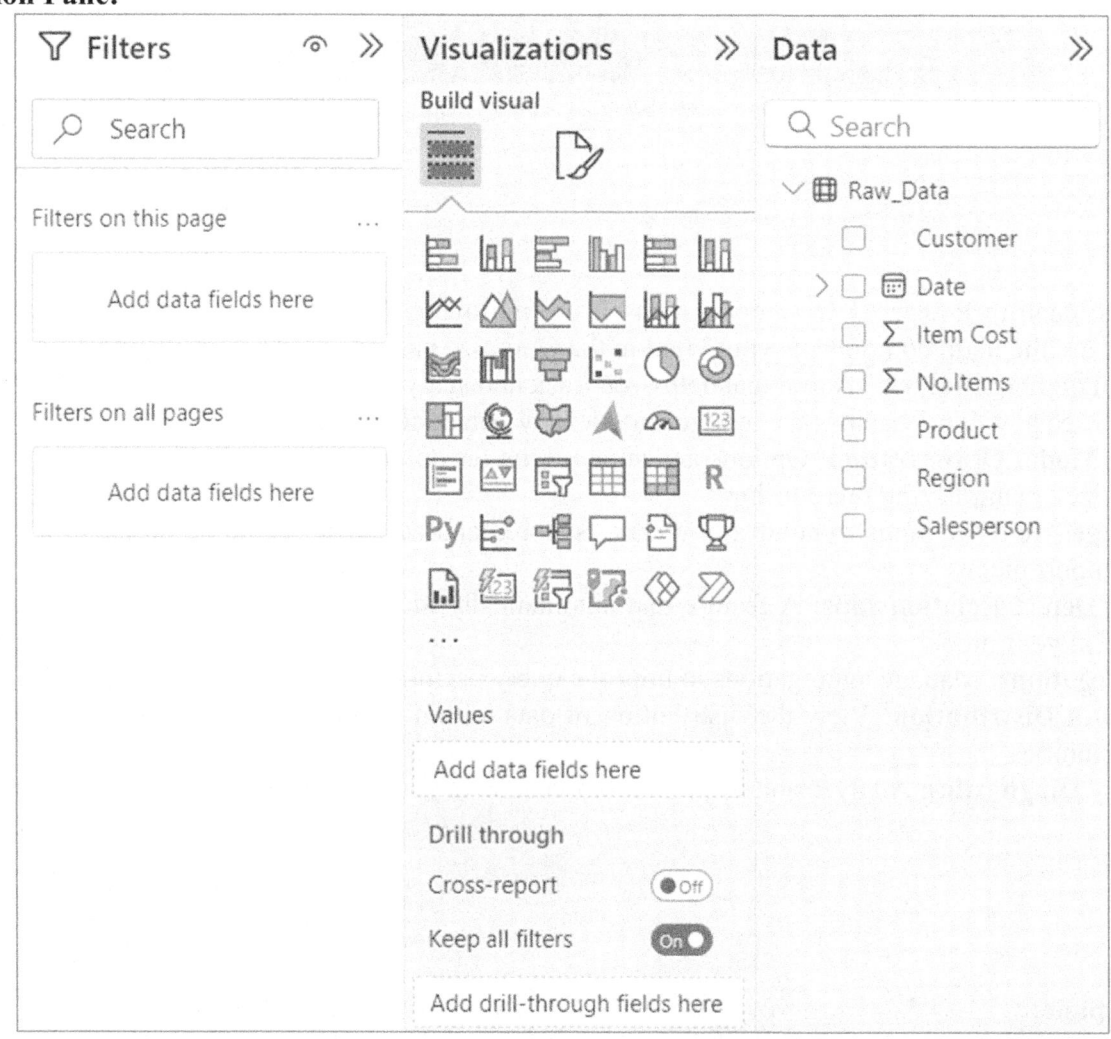

The Visualization pane in Power BI Desktop contains several key elements that facilitate the creation and customization of visualizations. Here are the main elements you'll find:
1. **Visuals Gallery**: A collection of visual types you can add to your report, including:
    - Bar and column charts
    - Line and area charts
    - Pie and donut charts
    - Tables and matrices
    - Maps (e.g., filled map, ArcGIS)
    - Card visuals
    - KPI visuals
    - Combo charts
    - Waterfall charts
2. **Fields Section**: Displays all the fields available in your data model. You can drag and drop these fields into your visuals to populate them with data.
3. **Filters Area**: This section allows you to apply filters to the selected visual or the entire report. You can drag fields here to filter data displayed in the visuals.
4. **Format Pane**: When you select a visual, this pane allows you to customize its appearance. You can adjust settings for:
    - Titles and labels
    - Data colors
    - Legends
    - Gridlines
    - Backgrounds
    - Borders
    - Data labels
5. **Visual Interactions**: Settings that control how visuals interact with one another. You can define which visuals filter others when selecting data points.
6. **Drillthrough**: This allows you to set up detailed drillthrough capabilities, enabling users to navigate to different report pages for more in-depth information based on selections.
7. **Tooltips**: Options for customizing what information appears in tooltips when users hover over elements in the visual.
8. **Conditional Formatting**: Settings to apply formatting rules based on specific conditions, enhancing the visual representation of data.

Chapter 4: Creating Visuals with Power BI